W9-BUW-489

STANDING UP TO LIFE

Clifford Norton

FRANK HALLIDAY FERRIS

Standing Up to Life

by

Frank Halliday Ferris

✠

The Bobbs-Merrill Company, Inc.

PUBLISHERS

INDIANAPOLIS NEW YORK

PRINTED IN THE UNITED STATES OF AMERICA

Library of Congress Catalog Card Number: 53-5231

First Edition

"Four Things" is reprinted from *The Poems of Henry van Dyke;* copyright 1911 by Charles Scribner's Sons, 1939 by Tertius van Dyke; used by permission of the publishers.

Lines from "Ultima Veritas" by Washington Gladden are reprinted by permission of The Pilgrim Press.

Lines from *Bees in Amber* by John Oxenham are reprinted by permission of American Tract Society, Inc. Copyright, 1908, by American Tract Society, Inc.

Lines from "Renascence" in *Renascence and Other Poems* published by Harper & Brothers. Copyright, 1912, 1940, by Edna St. Vincent Millay.

Chapter XIV was suggested by a portion of Paul Scherer's book *We Have This Treasure.*

Dedication

TO THE CONGREGATION OF FAIRMOUNT CHURCH

WHOSE STEADFAST ATTENTION AND CONSTANT ENCOURAGEMENT

HAVE HELPED ME TO BRING OUT THE BEST I HAD TO GIVE

CONTENTS

STANDING UP TO LIFE

Into Thy Hand

✠

O THOU in whose presence is fullness of joy, we come here in the faith that if we commit our way to thee, thou wilt show us the path of life and empower us to walk in it. We come because we believe that the life of man and the life of God are one, that a man never comes to himself until he comes to thee, that in opening ourselves to thine influence our deepest destiny is fulfilled. Thou art a God who hidest thyself. Thou dost not force thyself upon us. We have to seek thee. But when we find thee, we find that thou hast all the time been seeking us, that the prior quest is thine.

Some of us are young, awake to life's pleasures and thrills but unsaved from its perils. Help them to remember their Creator in the days of their youth before the evil days come; to keep themselves straight and clean, that their latter years may be free from the bitterness of regret.

Some are in middle life. On them fall most heavily the heat and burden of the day as they try to do their work well and carry their responsibilities without faltering. Show them that when even the youth faint and grow weary, they that wait on the Lord shall renew their strength and find it equal to their need.

Some are in the sunset hour, the heat and struggle past, the day's work done. O thou who makest the outgoings of the morning and evening to rejoice, fulfill in them the promise that at eventide there shall be light.

Some are worried, anxious, nervous, afraid. Remind them that thou hast not given us a spirit of fear but of power and love and self-control. Make them sure that whatever the morrow brings, it can bring with it nothing but thou wilt bear us through. Teach them to cast their care on thee, who carest for us.

Some are lonely and sad, so desolate they can hardly lift up their hearts even in this high hour. O thou who healest the broken in heart and bindest up their wounds, keep them beneath the covert of thy wing. Make known to them that though weeping may tarry for a night, joy cometh in the morning, that the darkness and the light are both alike to thee, that neither they nor those whom here they see no more can drift beyond thy love and care.

Some are in good health and spirit. We have food to eat and homes to shelter us, books to read and friends to love, music and art and nature to enjoy. May our gratitude for our good fortune take the form of a deep desire to serve our fellows, to help where help is needed, to befriend those who need our friendship most.

Young and old, happy and sad, we all alike need thee. Thou art our light and our salvation, our strength and our song. In thy hand are our times. In thy will is our peace. In thy fullness our little lives are made complete. Into thy hand we commend our spirits in Jesus' name. Amen.

I

Man's Hopes and Achievements

THE second epistle of Peter is one of the least known and least important books of the New Testament. But it has this interest: it is probably the latest of them, of all the Bible books the one that stands closest to us in time. And it has value as reflecting the mood of the time in which it was written.

More than a century had elapsed since Jesus' death. The first rapture, the first enthusiasm of the Christian movement had faded. Differences had arisen. The hope of a speedy return of Christ had waned. It was a day, the writer tells us, when mockers—and, we suspect, not only mockers but discouraged Christians as well—asked, "Where is the promise of his coming? For all things continue as they were."

Here is a note of frustration which finds an echo in many minds today. Not to weary you with historic background, let me say at once that all the political movements of the second century conspired to throw a cloud of gloom not only over Christians but over the pagans who lived side by side with them. Civilization itself seemed to hang in the balance. Men's hearts grew faint from fear.

"Where is the promise of his coming? For all things continue as they were." There is something peculiarly desolate in words like these from the second-century Christian community, because the Christian message had lifted men out of the idea which dominated ancient thought: that there is no such thing as progress, only cycles returning upon themselves to work out old situations as they had been worked out a thousand times before; no path leading toward a goal, just endless circles around which life moves like a circus horse in a ring, always coming back to where it started.

Stoicism, next to Christianity the noblest attitude toward life, is full of expressions of pessimism and futility, worthy of the jaded cynic who wrote Ecclesiastes with its recurrent "Vanity of vanities! All is vanity," its insistence that there is nothing new under the sun—it has all happened before. Seneca, Epictetus and Marcus Aurelius are high-minded moral guides, but the good life to which they summon men is unsustained by hope: fortitude and resignation are the virtues men need to face inexorable fate.

The religion of Jesus projected itself into the midst of the pagan world with a new hope, a belief in progress. The Christian no longer saw in human history a tale without a meaning, a battle without a victory, a voyage without a haven; there was a

> . . . far-off, divine event
> To which the whole creation moves.

Yet after the first flush of enthusiasm had subsided and hope deferred made the heart sick, men began to ask themselves whether perhaps the pagan was not right and the Christian wrong: "Where is the promise of his coming? For all things continue as they were."

We hear that note today. The scientific materialist tells us that the world begins in vapor, passes through a process of evolution and ends in smoke. Some of us have pinned our hopes to gradual improvement, the slow processes of education, long-range agencies like the United Nations. Today we find ourselves set back on our heels, our brave hopes gone a-glimmering. All things continue as they were. Where is the warless world, the kingdom of righteousness and peace of which we were talking so confidently and enthusiastically just a few years ago?

Look back again to the time when Second Peter was written. While some men were talking in this disconsolate way, while others were looking into the clouds for some catastrophic descent from heaven, simple, sincere Christians were leading simple, sincere Christian lives where they were and by their lives winning others to the faith, attacking the evils around them until gradually, here and there, the citadels of evil fell. Infanticide, once a common practice in the case of unwanted children, was ended; gladiatorial combats, once a favorite form of entertainment, were ended; the status of womanhood was raised from that of drudge or plaything to companion, as the implications of Jesus' teaching of the sacredness of human personality became clear.

In his *Adventures of Ideas,* Professor Alfred North Whitehead shows how during the first three Christian centuries under Christian impetus the idea of freedom began a triumphal march which has sometimes been checked but never stopped in all the intervening years. These fainthearted, discouraged men were wrong. All things did not continue as they were. Christ had not come on the clouds of heaven, but he had put into the souls of men a new spirit which would not tolerate ancient wrongs and which, as a contemporary opponent of Christianity acknowledged, enabled them to turn the world upside down.

Come closer to our own time. Those of you who are familiar with the history and literature of England in the eighteenth century know to what depths life had fallen when the four Georges sat upon the throne. The best of them was George III, whose obstinacy cost England her American colonies. The other three were libertines. Of the second it was said that he united the morals of a rake with the tastes of a boar. The Prime Minister, Sir Robert Walpole, lived a life of open profligacy. The upper classes were brazenly immoral, caring nothing for the miseries of the poor. The lower classes were brutalized, especially in the cities where they lived in physical and moral filth almost passing belief. Bull baiting, cockfighting and attending executions were the popular sports. Lord Ilchester lost eighteen hundred pounds dicing at a single dinner party. Hogarth painted his appalling picture of English life in "The Rake's Progress." Every sixth shop in London was a grog shop displaying such signs as "Drunk for a penny, dead drunk for two pence."

Irreligious as well as immoral was this deplorable period. A distinguished French visitor during the reign of George II noted that "when religion is mentioned in England, everyone laughs." Carlyle summarized the era in a withering phrase: "Soul extinct, body well alive."

Yet early in this century—on June 17, 1703—a baby was born in a country rectory, the fifteenth of nineteen children, of whom his mother wrote in her diary: "My son John . . . I do intend to be more particularly careful of the soul of this child."

At eleven we find him, a frail boy, running around the playground at Charterhouse before breakfast to keep fit; at seventeen he enters Oxford; at twenty-two he writes in his diary, "I spend an hour every day in religious meditation."

A few years later, when launched upon his work, it was his habit to rise at four, pray till five, preach from five to six to men on their way to work, write innumerable letters, organize his class meetings, preach again, an average of fifteen sermons a week, most of them in the open air. He continued to preach till within a week of his death, in his eighty-eighth year.

He was not of commanding appearance, but he said he made it a rule always to look a mob in the face. He traveled five thousand miles a year on horseback, his saddlebags full of books, studying his Hebrew Old Testament and Greek New Testament as he rode. He was accounted one of the most learned and best-read men of his day. He wrote a journal of 700,000 words which Augustine Birrell called "the most amazing record of human exertion ever penned." No man did more to foster and supply good reading tastes. He founded almost the first magazine. A stream of books poured from his pen. The royalties on them came to thirty thousand pounds, all of which he gave away. He provided work for the deserving poor, helped those who had been imprisoned for debt, opened dispensaries, was keenly interested in medicine and sanitation. He changed the moral climate. Some historians credit him with averting in England a replica of the French Revolution. When English life was at its lowest ebb there came—John Wesley.

We sometimes find ourselves in a mood of depression, almost of despair. The frightened victims of war, the millions on the verge of starvation, are never far from our thoughts. We are shocked by the impotence of religion to right the world's wrongs. It is humiliating to admit that Christianity after nineteen hundred years has made so little difference in that part of the world where it has long been the dominant religion. In the early days it was said of Christians that they turned the world upside down. It is now evident that, despite Christianity, the world has turned upside down again. We live in a pagan society, whose controlling ideas are the opposite of Christian, and this after nineteen centuries of Christian teaching.

"Where is the promise of his coming? For all things continue as they were." Not quite all. Slavery is gone. Dueling is gone. Human sacrifice is gone. Religious persecution is gone. Race prejudice is still with us, but an aroused conscience is arrayed against it. War is still with us, but never was war hated as it is today.

The reading of history, the gaining of historic perspective, is an antidote to the pessimism which declares that "all things continue as they were." It is true that many old problems remain unsolved, but each time we approach them we approach them on a higher level. Let a single illustration suffice. In Marquis James's biography of Andrew Jackson, he describes the funeral of one of Jackson's kinsmen. A diary records the amount of liquor consumed during the nights when friends sat up with the body. When the burial party reached the cemetery they found to their chagrin that the body of the deceased was missing. They were so drunk they had failed to notice that it had fallen off the sled several miles back.

Perhaps I should apologize for repeating such a grisly

story, which I do to point out one thing: alcoholism is still a major problem. It menaces our safety on the highways, takes heavy toll of broken lives and broken homes. No problem is ever settled till it is settled right, and this problem has not yet been settled right. But such an incident as the one recounted by Marquis James is unthinkable. All things are not quite as they were.

As we look out across a troublous world, let us face the facts but let us face all the facts. There is blackness, yes. But amid the blackness, babies are being born. And in this new life is the promise of a better day. Some of the babies born this year will be among the saviors of our race. Perhaps one will find a cure for cancer. Others will be pioneers and leaders in the field of race relationships, industrial relationships, international relationships. Others will have the gift of speech to influence the thoughts of men. Others will write songs that lift the heart and make it sing.

When I see a newborn baby I feel a thrill of elation. I ask myself, "Is this the one who will lead men into some new promised land? Is this the one who will help redeem this beautiful but shadowed world?"

Fantastic? No. I cited John Wesley. Come a little closer to our own day. In the early years of the last century Europe was in a stew. It was being overrun by a high-class thug named Napoleon. With bated breath men watched the career of this megalomaniac who bestrode Europe like a colossus. And all the while babies were being born. Look at some of these babies. Take a year midway between Trafalgar and Waterloo, the year the battle of Wagram was fought, the year 1809. In that year Gladstone was born in Liverpool and Lincoln on a Kentucky farm. Charles Darwin made his debut in Shrewsbury and Oliver Wendell Holmes opened his eyes on Cambridge, Massachusetts. Poetry was enriched by the advent of Tennyson at Somersby and Elizabeth Barrett at Durham, music by the birth of Frederic Chopin at Warsaw and Felix Mendelssohn at Hamburg. Nobody paid any attention to these babies except their families. Everyone's eyes were riveted on the battles being fought. But looking back from the vantage point of the present, it is easy to answer the question, Which mattered more, the battles of 1809 or the babies of 1809? Someday men will ask the same question and give the same answer concerning the battles and the babies of 1953.

When a wrong wants righting or a work wants doing or a truth wants preaching, God sends a baby into the world. So it was that once in Bethlehem of Judea a babe was born.

✠

Prayer

O THOU who hast made all ages a preparation for the advent of thy son, above the tumult of our world may his voice sound clear, speaking the word of reconciliation and of peace.

Renew within us the high, prophetic anticipation of our holy faith. Dwell in us where fear and care have dwelt too long. Attune our lives to the promise of his coming in whom thou art reconciling the world to thyself.

May his grace abide in every heart and home. Amen.

II

A King in Three Languages

When Jesus was nailed to the cross there was nailed to it also above his head a title which Pilate had written. In the synoptics it is called a superscription, but John uses the technical term. The titulus or title was the board bearing the name of the condemned man and the name of his crime. This was the title Pilate wrote: "Jesus of Nazareth, the King of the Jews." It was a deliberate insult, a sneer, a sardonic jest, the retaliation of a proud man who found himself helpless in the hands of people he despised and by them forced to do what he knew was wrong. And he stuck to it despite their protest. One can imagine a gleam of satisfaction lighting up his gloomy face when the chief priests came begging him to change what he had written—and he knew his taunt had told.

"Do not write 'the King of the Jews,' but 'This man said, I am King of the Jews.' "

Pilate answered, "What I have written I have written."

The title was written in three languages so that all who had come to Jerusalem for the passover might read it. Such multilingual inscriptions were common in the Roman provinces: they were written in Greek, the universal language, in Latin, the official language, and in the native language of the province, in this case Hebrew or the current dialect derived from it, Aramaic. Some could read it in one language, some in two (there were many bilinguals in Palestine and the Mediterranean world), some in all three.

Such was the intent of the threefold title, but in writing it in these three tongues Pilate did better than he knew. For in their influence on Western civilization, these are the three classical languages of antiquity. Each stands for a distinct idea, was the vehicle of a distinctive genius. Greek was the language of culture, Latin the language of power, Hebrew the language of religion. Do you see what Pilate did when in mockery he wrote the threefold title, "Jesus of Nazareth, the King of the Jews"? He proclaimed Jesus king in the realm represented by the Greek language, the kingdom of the mind; he proclaimed Jesus king in the realm represented by the Latin language, the kingdom of the will; he proclaimed Jesus king in the realm represented by the Hebrew tongue, the kingdom of the heart.

Pilate wrote a title and put it on the cross and it was written in Greek, the language of culture, of thought. In the Athens of the Golden Age of Pericles—in the fifth century before Christ—man's intellectual development reached a point it had never reached before and in the fields of art, literature and philosophy has never reached since. Men speak of "the glory that was Greece." What was this glory but the wealth of beauty produced by this little Mediterranean land which has permanently enriched the world? In art the Greek genius came to flower in the unrivaled sculptures of Phidias and Praxiteles. In poetry the Greek genius burst into song in the epics of Homer, the odes of Pindar, the lyrics of Sappho. In philosophy the Greek mind scaled the heights of human wisdom in the *Dialogues* and *Republic* of Plato, in the *Ethics* and *Politics* of Aristotle. In drama the Greek imagination produced the tragedies of Aeschylus, Sophocles and Euripides, the comedies of Aristophanes.

It was a many-sided genius, flowering not in one but in many forms of beauty. Alexander, setting out to conquer the world, could tell his teacher Aristotle that it was his intent "to make all men everywhere Greeks." For he himself was so imbued with the Greek spirit that he could think of no greater benefit he could confer on mankind than to make them sharers in it. He succeeded in making Greek the language of the civilized world, in diffusing throughout it a knowledge of Greek culture. And all this treasure house of culture was represented at the cross. It was written in Greek, "This is the king." Jesus claims the realm of thought, the kingdom of beauty, for his own.

Pilate wrote a title and put it on the cross and it was written in Latin, the language of power, of conquest, of dominion, of law and government. From their city on the Tiber, throned upon its seven hills, the Romans ruled the then known world and ruled it well—a larger proportion and a greater variety of the human race than have ever been under one rule. So far as numbers go, China, Russia, the British Empire before it relinquished India, far exceed it; for the world's population is vastly larger than when Rome was at the zenith of its power. But there was a peculiar unity about the Roman Empire in that it embraced, so men thought, all civilized mankind. When Augustus died in 14 A.D. it covered 3,340,000 square miles, an area larger than the United States, a hundred times the area of Rome before the Punic Wars. It stretched from the forests of Germany to the heart of Africa—

2,000 miles; from the British Isles to the Tigris-Euphrates—3,000 miles.

Where Roman legions with their eagle standards led, Roman colonists followed. Roman engineers laid out the sturdy Roman roads, some of which are still in use, the trade routes that linked the farthest outposts of empire together, all of them converging on the capital city, so that it was literally true that all roads led to Rome. Roman jurists developed the Roman law, on which all legal systems since have been modeled. A general peace prevailed throughout the Roman world—the Pax Romana, which Will Durant calls the supreme achievement in the annals of statesmanship. For 200 years from Augustus to Antoninus Pius, roughly coinciding with the first two centuries of our era, it gave the Mediterranean world order and tranquillity; gave men a chance to think, undistracted by the tumult of war. Milton in his stately "Ode on the Morning of Christ's Nativity" alludes to the fact that when Jesus was born

> No war or battle's sound
> Was heard the world around.

There had never been a general peace before; there has rarely been one since.

The Roman citizen enjoyed a large measure of freedom. The Roman rule allowed a maximum of local self-government, respected local customs and traditions. Rome ruled—so one of its poets declared—more like a mother than a queen. Men were proud of their Roman citizenship. If "the glory that was Greece" was its culture, "the grandeur that was Rome" was its genius for government. This genius was represented at the cross. It was written in Latin, "This is the king." Jesus claims this realm also as his own.

Pilate wrote a title and put it on the cross and it was written in Hebrew, the language of religion, the language of the heart. The little country which gave this language to the world had little of the culture of Greece, none of the imperialism of Rome. It was the plaything of the great military powers by which it was surrounded and by which again and again it was overrun—the cockpit of the ancient world as Belgium was the cockpit of Europe at the time of Napoleon and again in 1914 and 1940. When mighty armies marched against each other, again and again it was on Palestinian soil that the battle was joined.

Israel had no distinction in any of the realms which the world deems great. Yet this obscure people was chosen to give to the world the knowledge of God. Its mission began about two thousand years before Christ when Abraham set out from Ur of the Chaldees, not knowing whither he went, knowing only that God had called him. Later, about 1200 B.C., Moses organized a disorderly rabble of slaves into some semblance of a nation, a nation governed by the laws of God. Later came the prophets, that unique line of religious teachers without parallel in history: the earliest, Amos, declaring that God is a righteous God who cares nothing for ceremony, everything for justice and righteousness; his contemporary, Hosea, proclaiming God's tender mercy and forgiving love; another, the princely Isaiah, catching a vision of the majesty of God and crying, "Holy, holy, holy is the Lord of hosts; the whole earth is full of his glory"; another, the unknown prophet of the exile, impressed by the power and the patience of God: "Lift up your eyes on high and see:

who created these? He who brings out their host by number, calling them all by name; by the greatness of his might, and because he is strong in power not one is missing. . . . Have you not known? Have you not heard? The Lord is the everlasting God, the Creator of the ends of the earth. He does not faint or grow weary, his understanding is unsearchable. He gives power to the faint, and to him who has no might he increases strength." (Isaiah 40:26, 28.)

Through priest and prophet, singer and sage, Israel bequeathed its legacy to the world—the knowledge of the true and living God. Even its books of history are permeated with the sense of God and his control of human destiny, the conviction that God has a purpose for men and that his will expects consent. All the resources of its rugged and sonorous language were employed to proclaim this truth. To this day the devout Jew summons his last energies, his dying breath, to repeat the words taught him as a child: "Hear, O Israel: the Lord our God is one Lord; and you shall love the Lord your God with all your heart, and with all your soul, and with all your might." (Deuteronomy 6:4.) The genius of Greece was culture, of Rome government, of Israel religion. This too was represented at the cross. It was written in Hebrew, "This is the king." Jesus claims the realm of religion for his own.

These three languages in which the title on the cross was written have a more personal significance. The Greek may well stand for the mind of man, the Latin for the will of man, the Hebrew for the heart of man. Together they proclaim Jesus the lord and saviour of the whole man. He alone can control our thought life, from which our words and actions spring. He alone can control our will with all its fickleness, can make us strong to bring our will into harmony with the will of God. He alone can control our affections, until all that is within us responds to the love that called us into being and has surrounded us all our days.

Each of these three, the Greek, the Latin and the Hebrew, by itself stands for incompleteness and failure.

Greece with its philosophy, its cult of beauty, appeals to the intellectual and the aesthete but exerts slight influence on the common man. Mere mental development, for which Greece stands, is inadequate to human need. Philosophy is a feeble defense before the onslaughts of passion. Art for art's sake is often an enervating rather than a strengthening influence on character. A former warden of Sing Sing asserted that among his charges were men capable of teaching every subject in a university curriculum; yet, so far from being an asset to society, they were so much of a liability that society was obliged to restrain them for its own protection.

Intelligence and education by themselves are not enough. Every one of us knows that his mind needs control. Just as a watch must be synchronized with standard time before it is of any use as a timekeeper, so our thought life, our mental energies, our intellectual development need to be related to eternal truth. Else our minds will lead us astray, as the will-o'-the-wisp leads the traveler into the marshy quicksand to his doom.

The disintegration and decay of the Roman Empire, which at the time of Christ looked impregnable and as permanent as the earth itself, typifies the failure and inadequacy of secular power. Its resplendent pomp rests upon a fragile lease. Historians tell us now that the fall of Rome was not caused by the attacks of Vandals, Goths, Visigoths and Huns: their coming into the Italian peninsula was in the nature of successive waves of immigration which the already enfeebled Romans were too weak to resist. The fall of Rome was occasioned by the disintegration of the Roman character as a result of Rome's material aggrandizement and the enervating effects of the luxury and corruption which followed in its train.

So today a man's real foes are not without but within, and this is never so true as when he has won some measure of material success. The strongest will breaks down in the hour when we need it most. Mere stubbornness of purpose is not enough. Unless the will is subject to a higher control, it may be as dangerous as a high-powered car with a drunken driver. Who of us can order his own will? Today, under the influence of this place and hour, you will to be good, you will to be true; but tomorrow, when you are surrounded by a different set of influences, your resolution evaporates, your will is overborne. Just as your mind needs to be brought under control of the mind of Christ, so your will needs the control offered in his invitation, "Follow me."

The downfall of the Hebrew nation typifies the failure of that for which the Hebrew language stands. For the heart of man is like a ship: it must steer by something outside itself, more stable and dependable than itself. Otherwise its instability can bring only disaster. As the mind and will need control, so the heart with all its passions and desires needs control.

And Christ can give us the control we need.

In his solution of our intellectual problems he is sovereign of the mind. All the deep and final questions of sin, of suffering, of conscience, of judgment, of the future life are illumined by him. What philosophy only guesses at or endlessly discusses, what philosophy punctuates by a question mark, Jesus calmly declares. He may not tell us all we want to know; he does tell us all we need to know. He declares as open secrets things sealed for ages from the wisdom of men and reveals to little children things hidden from the learned, the clever and the subtle. To the Greeks he declares, "I am the truth"; not "I speak the truth" nor "I am an aspect of the truth" nor "I am a mediator of the truth" but "I am the truth." It has been well said that Christ by his words taught the gospel, that Christ by his life and death made the gospel, but that Christ is the gospel. And I say to you people with your keen intellectual curiosity, with the irritation set up in your minds by the complex problems of modern life, that this Jesus whose title is written in Greek can so guide and direct your mind as to leave it in no doubt about final and essential things, can make your intellect an efficient instrument in God's service.

As he is sovereign of the mind, so also he is lord of the will. He is lord of the will because he can subdue it and bring about its commitment to the will of him in whose will is our peace. He saves us from the "I won't" attitude when confronted by divine commands, the "I shan't" attitude when challenged by divine appeals. He puts behind the drive of our will a motivation that will save it from breaking down in the hour of stress or becoming enfeebled in the day of prosperity.

And he is king of the heart because he is the fulfillment of the heart's quest. Running through the Hebrew scriptures as the theme song runs through an opera—in the sacrifices of the altar, in the sermons of the prophets and the songs of the psalmists, above all in the Messianic hope which discouragement and disaster were powerless to quench—is the longing for an ideal sacrifice, an ideal prophet, an ideal king. Isaiah voices that longing in words of undying beauty in the second, ninth and eleventh chapters of the book which bears his name. This same longing for an ideal prophet, priest and king to whom we can give our full allegiance is hidden in our hearts. Jesus comes to meet that longing, the incarnate love of God, by whom and in whom the heart of God is revealed. To the Greek mind he says, "I am the truth." To the Roman will he declares, "I am the way." To the Hebrew heart with its longing for goodness and for God he proclaims, "I am the life."

In letters of Greek and Latin and Hebrew he makes his claim today. How far have you recognized his claim? How real is the faith you profess in him? For your faith is not what you hold; it is what holds you. It is expressed not in terms of belief but in terms of loyalty. We do not know Christ at all until we know him as lord of our lives, our minds, our wills, our hearts. That is what it means to be a Christian.

In a day when would-be Caesars and diminutive Napoleons, riding at the head of their armies, make their triumphal entries into the cities of their vanquished foes, we celebrate the triumphal entry of the king of love and prince of peace. To be sure, his triumph was short-lived. Before the week was out he had been seized, tried, killed. But brief as it was, it serves as a promise and a presage of the day when hate and error will have been conquered, when love and truth shall reign supreme. Can one believe in God and not believe in the eventual triumph of the Christ? Someday he will make his entry into the cities of the world, into the city of Mansoul, not to be crucified but to be enthroned.

Lift up your eyes and see him afresh over whom this threefold title was written. See him with the mark of the nails in his hands and feet, with the gash in his side where the spear was driven in. See him with the crown of thorns pushed down upon his brow. Then take the crown of your life—your mind, your will, your heart—and place it upon his brow so that it hides the scars by which we were redeemed: "Bring forth the royal diadem and crown him—crown him lord of all!"

✠

Prayer

O THOU in whom and by whom we live, Source of the light that never fades, the love that never fails, the life that never ends, who hast set within us a spirit which answers to thine own, we gather here to commune with thee, to express our gratitude for the past and our hope for the morrow.

We thank thee for sweet and hallowed memories, for the homes from which we came, for the friends whose devotion we have proved, for those who loved us better than they loved themselves, for the wealth bequeathed to us by the past. No other age has been heir to so much knowledge, beauty, power. Poets, prophets, artists, scholars, men of science have laid their gifts at our feet. We rejoice in the beauty created by man's hand and brain and in the vaster beauty created by thee, in nature bursting forth in bud and flower, in the good earth which nourishes our souls with beauty as it feeds our bodies with bread.

O thou in whom our fathers trusted, we thank thee that thou who hast never forsaken thy children art still our refuge and our strong tower. It is not always easy to hold onto our courage and self-control, to keep faith with our fellows, to maintain the integrity of our own souls. Tomorrow we shall go out again into a difficult world. Tomorrow we shall be part of a society which often appeals to our worst. Tomorrow we shall be tempted to think that amid the handicaps and hardships of the time we cannot get out the best that is in us. Tomorrow we are likely to forget that difficult days bring out the weakness of the weak and the strength of the strong and that some never bring out the best that is in them until they face a struggle against odds. Tomorrow that test is going to fall on some of us. Help us to meet it. Through Jesus Christ our Lord. Amen.

III

Four Rules of Life

"BY WHAT long discipline and at what cost," says Thoreau in his journal, "a man learns to speak simply at last." In my younger days I tried to write learned articles, garnished with classical allusions and studded with gems from such heavy thinkers as John Dewey and Bertrand Russell, Toynbee and Sorokin, Reinhold Niebuhr and Jacques Maritain.

Now when I am asked to write something, I make it as simple as I can, because the simpler it is, the better its chance of being remembered, especially if it has a simple and easily remembered outline. The outline of this is based on a familiar stanza entitled "Four Things." If I had written it, you'd call it doggerel; since Henry van Dyke wrote it, let's call it verse. I shall repeat it several times, commenting on each of the four things in turn. When I am through, you will unconsciously have memorized it and be able to ruminate on it yourself whenever it comes back to you and you associate it with this hour:

Four things a man must learn to do
If he would make his record true:
To think without confusion clearly;

> To love his fellowmen sincerely;
> To act from honest motives purely;
> To trust in God and Heaven securely.

I.

To think without confusion clearly.

To think clearly, we need something to exercise our minds upon. Facts are the raw material of thinking, which is why we need content courses as well as method courses, why we need to go on learning facts as long as we live if we aspire to be educated men. Of course we can learn only a fraction of them.

Of Aristotle, who lived in the fourth century B.C., it may truly be said that he had an encyclopedic mind. It was generally believed that he knew everything there was to know. His treatises on many and diverse subjects give ground for this belief and justify his title, "The father of those who know."

The last man for whom the claim is made that he knew everything there was to know was Roger Bacon, who lived in the thirteenth century. The learned friar took all knowledge for his province, all philosophy, every science; like Aristotle, wrote with equal erudition in various fields; is often called the father of the scientific method because of his emphasis on experiment as the door to knowledge and the criterion of truth.

Since Aristotle and especially since Roger Bacon, the expansion of knowledge has forced men to become specialists. No one can compass a single field as did Edward Gibbon, John

Locke or Adam Smith. It takes a lifetime to master a minute part of a science such as enzymes in organic chemistry, stratiography in geology or genetics in biology. Sir Isaac Newton (1642-1727) said he seemed to himself like a boy, picking up pebbles on the seashore, while before him lay the great ocean of undiscovered truth.

A man can no longer know everything or even a little about everything. Woodrow Wilson, a first-rate educator, suggested as an attainable ideal a general knowledge of what men have thought and done; that is, a general knowledge of the history of the world and the history of ideas, a working knowledge of one science and of one language, preferably one's own. This is a modest objective. Anyone who keeps slogging along through the years can reach it. In addition, an educated man knows how to extend the horizon of his competence in any direction that becomes necessary. He knows that there is no occult knowledge; it is all freely accessible. If he needs more information on any subject, he has only to go to the nearest library. My own method for many years has been to write the leading authority in any field I wanted to look into and ask for guidance. The bigger the man, the more careful and courteous his reply.

We cannot know it all, as Aristotle did, yet in a day of specialization, when vocational training has largely preempted the educational world, we make a mistake if we narrow ourselves too far. If a young man is planning to be a writer, a lawyer or a minister, he does well to take at least a few courses in the exact sciences, to learn the austere beauty of factual precision. If all ministers had this kind of training, there would be less loose thinking and loose talking from our pulpits. If a young man is planning to be a physicist, a chemist, a biologist, an engineer, for the good of his soul he should learn something about history, literature and the fine arts, instead of merely continuing to learn more and more about less and less. One of the saddest epitaphs ever chiseled on a gravestone was "Born a man, died a grocer." It would have been no less sad had it read, "Born a man, died a technician."

I have emphasized the value of facts as the raw material of thinking, but there is food for thought in an Oxford don's definition of education as "what you have left when you've forgotten all you learned." What have you left as the result of serious mental effort? A disciplined and informed intelligence, a critical faculty able to separate the essential from the unessential in a chaotic mass of facts, the ability to penetrate to the heart of a subject, the power and habit of reflection, a mind that is the foe of sophistry, of quick and easy generalizations, an appreciation of the fact that man has come a long way from crude and savage beginnings, that what he has slowly and painfully learned is entitled to respect but subject to continual correction and addition.

We can no longer say what an educated man should know. We can say what an educated man should be. He should be able to think without confusion clearly.

2.

Four things a man must learn to do
If he would make his record true:
To think without confusion clearly;
To love his fellowmen sincerely.

Love, you say, is an emotion. You either love a person or you don't. It is not something a man can learn to do. Certainly love is an ambiguous word, tied up in our minds with all kinds of sentimental and even unwholesome connotations. Shelley begins one of his poems, "One word is too often profaned for me to profane it": the word was love.

The Greek language, which, despite its smaller vocabulary, is more precise than ours, has three words for love. One is *philia,* the love between friends. This word occurs once in the New Testament (James 4:4), where it is used in a disparaging sense of love of the world. Another is *eros,* whence our words *erotic, eroticism.* This is the instinctive, almost physical, emotion which unites man and woman, mother and child. It may be a life-transforming passion but it cannot be produced at will. This word never occurs in the New Testament.

The New Testament word for love is *agape,* which is not primarily an emotion but a fixed attitude of good will, a deliberate acceptance of the fact that God has no favorites, no step-children; he loves every soul that he has made, sends his rain on the just and the unjust, makes his sun shine on the evil and the good with impartial benignity. He loves man as man, and it is our business to be like him. This is the essence of every high form of religion: be like God, reproduce in yourself his attitude and character; and God, affirms the New Testament, is love.

Love in the New Testament sense is no discriminating affection for an individual or a group. It is the will to do good, the consistent purpose to bless others, not to wound them. This helps to explain two commandments over which many have stumbled. One is the New Commandment: "A new commandment I give to you, that you love one another." "You cannot command love," you object. "A man cannot say to his son, 'I want you to fall in love with this girl; she'll make you a fine wife.' It doesn't happen that way." If you speak of love as an emotion, you cannot command it. If you think of it as a habitual attitude toward others, you can. You can cultivate it as you cultivate courtesy or consideration or any other flower that grows in the garden of the soul.

The other is what is sometimes called the impossible commandment: "Love your enemies and pray for those who persecute you." No one needs be told that it is impossible to love our enemies or indeed those outside our immediate circle as we love our family and our friends. What we can do is regard our enemies and all other human beings and even the subhuman creation with the steady resolve to do the best we can for them and never to allow the poison of hate to destroy our good will. A young Japanese, who had been a Japanese flier during the war, recently graduated from an American college. He was educated with the proceeds of a government insurance policy which came to the parents of one of our fliers, killed over Japan, who decided to use the money in this way. That is what it means to love your enemies.

If love be construed as self-giving, both as applied to God and to us, as that which seeks the highest good of its object, then one can make it his deliberate aim to love his fellow man sincerely. It is this kind of love, not romantic love, which Paul extols in the exalted paean which has sung its way down the centuries, beginning, "If I speak in the tongues of men and of angels but have not love, I am a noisy gong or a clanging cymbal," and ending, "Faith, hope, love abide; but the greatest of these is love."

I sometimes read the thirteenth chapter of First Corinthians in a personal way. Do I want to be eloquent, to be able to persuade men's minds and enlist their wills by the power of speech? Eloquence, unless motived by the will to benefit men, is a curse, as the demagogues of all ages have abundantly proved. Do I want to be learned, to master one segment of knowledge till I am thoroughly at home in it, then add a broad culture which will save me from the narrowness of specialization? It is a worthy ambition if kept free from intellectual pride; but learning, unless motived by the will to benefit men, is as arid as the Sahara. Do I want to be generous? Knowing how the spirit of acquisitiveness shrivels the soul and that I cannot depend on my spontaneous generous impulses—they're too few and far between—I may set myself a dogged program of giving. But unless my giving is motived by love . . . You know the saying, "as cold as charity."

Unless our giving is self-giving, our gifts are little worth. As Lowell says, "The gift without the giver is bare." Before you go to bed tonight, open your New Testament to this chapter and go through it clause by clause, taking it to yourself in this personal way. When you're through, you'll find yourself in a mood where it will not be hard to pray.

In sundry callings man fulfills his allotted years, but his work abides only when it is wrought in love. It is not an emotion to begin with, this love on which the New Testament dwells, but it becomes an emotion in the end. Who can look upon his fellow beings, their unadvertised courage, patience, sacrifice, the difficulties and disadvantages under which so many of them labor, their gallant highheartedness in face of them, without being deeply moved and proud to belong to such a race? That emotion is sound, sounder than the clever and corrosive cynicism which pollutes the air we breathe. Santayana, himself an intellectual, is everlastingly right:

> It is not wisdom to be only wise,
> But it is wisdom to believe the heart.

Therefore, "keep your heart with all vigilance; for from it flow the springs of life."

3.

This leads to the third thing

> ... a man must learn to do
> If he would make his record true:
> To think without confusion clearly;
> To love his fellowmen sincerely;
> *To act from honest motives purely.*

Motive and emotion come from the same root, the Latin verb meaning "to move." The springs of action are deeper than the reason. Our conduct is influenced by what we know but not determined by it. We tend to overestimate the power of knowledge. "Give people the facts," we say. "If they are informed, they will do what is right." It does not always follow. Facts in themselves have no moral compulsion.

Never has there been so much knowledge. Never has it

been so freely available. There are public libraries everywhere, containing more books than we can read. More information reaches us over the radio and through the mail than we can digest. What is America's biggest business? Steel? No. Agriculture? No. Education. Over one fifth of our total population are school people, teachers and taught. At the turn of the century there were 200,000 students in our colleges and universities. Now there are more than 2,000,000. The aristocratic tradition of education in this country was weakening before the war. The G.I. Bill of Rights gave it its deathblow. No matter which side of the track one is born on, the avenues of education are open as far as he is prepared to follow them.

An English schoolman, Headmaster Donald F. Taylor, points out that in Britain public education began as a charity and still carries the marks of its origin; that only since 1902 have local governments been empowered to provide post-primary schooling, only since 1944 been required by law to do so; that in England only one out of 660 students reaches a university, while in this country the ratio is one in 100. Our free system of education from kindergarten to university is the most democratic thing in America.

But knowledge without sound motivation profits nothing. A few years ago a man died in New York who was known as Columbia's perpetual student. I read his obituary in the *New York Times* with interest, for he had been in one of my classes. He was pointed out as a landmark even then. A wealthy relative had left him an annuity, payable until he finished his studies at Columbia. He never finished. Once he feared he would run out of courses, but in the nick of time the university expanded its curriculum. He accumulated more degrees than Nicholas Murray Butler, Columbia's distinguished president. He put none of his knowledge to use.

Knowledge seems to have little to do with moral progress, moral control. The fact that a man knows what is wrong does not always deter him from doing it. Knowledge makes an unscrupulous man a greater menace. If knowledge were a panacea, every university graduate would be a paragon of virtue. The hope of the world would be its learned men. The solution of its social problems from alcoholism to war would lie in the realm of education. Knowledge is indispensable, but it is not enough.

What is the most important thing in a man? Skill is highly desirable. We admire those who possess it. Sometimes we envy them. The old Roman ideal, a sound mind in a sound body, is highly desirable. Physical and mental vigor give a man self-confidence, inspire confidence in others. A genial, magnetic personality is a great asset. We know those who possess it in high degree. How easily they get along with people! How easily they draw people to them! But the most important quality in a man is none of these. The most important quality is integrity. Without it, everything else he has—his skill, his vigor, his charm—is subject to heavy discount.

To live with a man, to work by his side, you must be able to trust him. You may sometimes question his judgment, you may disagree with his opinions, you may even dislike him; it need not keep you from working with him. You may oppose him and still respect him. But if once you lose faith in his integrity, you can no longer walk with him. Your confidence has been destroyed.

What this country needs most is not, as a former Vice-President quipped, a good five-cent cigar nor, as someone else suggested, a reducing diet with a whipped-cream base. What this country needs most is morally reliable citizens,

> Men whom the lust of office does not kill;
> Men whom the spoils of office cannot buy.

A young deputy sheriff was the state's key witness in a certain case. Just before it came to trial, a man walked into his office and without a word put a roll of bills on his desk. And without a word, he threw the man out of his office and his money after him. What can you do to a boy to make him that kind of man? I wish I knew. Example helps, the example of those he loves and admires and whose approval he wants. The will can be strengthened by repeated right choices. And there is such a thing as conscience, though it is hard for a philosopher or a psychologist to say what it is. Dr. Fosdick tells of a boy who asked his father, "What is conscience?" "I don't know, son" was the reply, "but when that bell rings, you pick up the receiver." But the strongest of motivations comes from religion, which leads us to our fourth point.

4.

> Four things a man must learn to do
> If he would make his record true:
> To think without confusion clearly;
> To love his fellowmen sincerely;
> To act from honest motives purely;
> *To trust in God and Heaven securely.*

What does that mean? It means that at the heart of every experience, however baffling and mysterious, there is an unseen Presence to show us the meaning of it, to illumine the path where our next step will fall, to hold us up, to guide us through. This in a sentence is the religious interpretation of life. In this conviction religious men of all ages and whatever creed are one.

The great strength of the religious interpretation of life is that there is no satisfying alternative to it. Epicureanism, "Let us eat and drink for tomorrow we die"? As Dorothy Parker points out, we may not die and tomorrow we shall have a headache. Stoicism, to grit our teeth and "bear what is ordained with patience"? There is something admirable about unyielding courage, even when unsustained by hope, but it puts little meaning into life and little joy.

Secularism? Someone has defined it as "the organization of life apart from God." Men in many walks are beginning to suspect that when they try to organize life apart from God they have left out something essential, like trying to make bread without flour. The leading article in a recent issue of *Harvard Business Review* is entitled "Religion and the Business Man." It is by a professor in Harvard's prestigious School of Business Administration. He advances his views tentatively: you would not expect a Harvard professor to be a fanatic. But it is plain that he thinks the profit motive is not enough nor is the service motive, where service is construed merely as a device for getting more business. His implication is that the businessman needs a philosophy which will tie life together for him, keep it from going dead on him when human relations in his business become tense or profits decline.

The only fruitful way to think of life in any calling is as a trust committed to us by God, in which we try to put the talents given us, be they many or few, to fullest use under God's eye and with his help. Santayana defines piety as a reverent attachment to the sources of our being and the steadying of life by that attachment. I do not know what else can steady life in this tumultuous age.

The assiduous Dr. Gallup reports that ninety-six per cent of the American people believe in God. We have learned that a Gallup poll is not infallible, but another survey conducted by the *Ladies' Home Journal* arrives at approximately the same result. It is reassuring to know that ninety-six per cent of our fellow citizens believe in God. But there is a difference between belief in God as a first cause, an explanation of the universe, and faith in God as the power that makes for righteousness.

What does faith in God mean? Let me try to tell you in simplest words.

It means that the universe is on our side, that God did not create it and us to amuse himself, that he has a purpose and a plan, conceived in and controlled by love. This is the faith we need to deliver us from the haunting sense of futility, the faith which gives dignity and meaning to life.

It means that divine resources are available to us. We do not think of goodness, truth, justice as resources. We think of them as ideals and from our point of view they are. But when we think of them in relation to God, they are realities, resources on which we can draw. When we put ourselves in line with them, we are in tune with the infinite. When we try to run counter to them, the stars in their courses are arrayed against us. You can no more successfully resist them than you can defy the law of gravitation or stand in the way of a ten-ton truck. Faith in God means believing in spiritual resources, trusting them, allying yourself with them, sure that in the long run they are bound to win, saying with Washington Gladden that

> . . . fierce though the fiends may fight,
>   And long though the angels hide,
> I know that Truth and Right
>   Have the universe on their side;
>
> And that somewhere, beyond the stars,
>   Is a Love that is better than fate;
> When the night unlocks her bars
>   I shall see Him, and I will wait.

And faith in God means doing what God wants us to do. This is the crux of personal religion. In one of George MacDonald's novels the hero goes off by himself with a New Testament, bent on finding the secret of the Christian religion. After three days he returns to report that it boils down to three propositions:

> It is a man's business to do the will of God.
> It is God's business to take care of that man.
> And therefore a man should never be afraid of anything.

It would be hard to improve on that as a three-point summary of the teaching of Jesus. Note which stands first: it is a man's business to do the will of God. This is where religion for us begins. It ends in knowing Him, whom to know is life eternal.

To think without confusion clearly;
To love his fellowmen sincerely;
To act from honest motives purely;
To trust in God and Heaven securely:
These things a man must learn to do
If he would make his record true.

Prayer

GOD FORBID that we should take lightly a religion that brought its founder to a cross. God give us something of his purpose and passion, that we may do his work and help bring the world back to what it was meant to be. God save us from living frivolous lives in so desperate a time. God help us to live in the deeps of our natures, to think and will and do as they must think and will and do who take Jesus in earnest. Amen.

IV

It Tolls for Thee

One of the curious and colorful figures of English literature is John Donne. "For evil and for good," says the Cambridge History, "Donne is the most shaping and determining influence that meets us in passing from the sixteenth to the seventeenth century."

He is called "the metaphysical poet" because he loved to look at common things through the smoked glasses of metaphysics, but he first made his reputation as a writer of love lyrics. He wrote also elegiac, satirical and religious poems, philosophical, controversial and devotional prose. He was accounted the greatest wit of his age, *wit* at that time meaning not a jester but a man of perspicacity, of intellectual acumen, who could express his insights in a telling and memorable way.

Shortly after his death, Izaak Walton wrote an admirable biography of him. A more recent one is by Edmund Gosse. Gosse declares that Donne's influence on English literature was "wide and deep and almost wholly malign," but pays tribute to his vigorous mind, flashing imagination and insight into spiritual mysteries.

Donne lived from 1573 to 1631, which means that he was a younger contemporary of Shakespeare (1564-1616), born in the reign of Elizabeth, living through the reign of James I into that of Charles I. His early career was a checkered one. You will find something about him in Lytton Strachey's *Elizabeth and Essex,* for he sailed with Essex (Robert Devereux, 2nd Earl of Essex) on the *Repulse* to Cadiz and the Azores, in the naval expeditions against the Spaniards.

In his forty-second year, convinced that every other path to preferment was closed, Donne entered the ministry. He quickly gained great popularity as a preacher, which continued till his death at the age of fifty-eight. He preached to the intelligentsia at Lincoln's Inn. He preached before the king at Whitehall. In 1621 King James made him dean of St. Paul's where his fame reached its height and fashionable London flocked to hear him. One of his contemporaries asserts that his sermon was the most exciting event of the week.

In his preaching, as earlier in his poems, he was preoccupied with the thought of death, warning in solemn tones of that which "comes equally to us all and makes us all equal when it comes." Six weeks before his death he rose from a sickbed to preach his last sermon. Its title was "Death's Duel." He then posed for his statue, standing before a fire in his study, his winding sheet wrapped around him, his eyes shut, his feet resting on a funeral urn. This lugubrious work of art was set up in white marble in St. Paul's, where it may still be seen.

However questionable the motives which took him into the ministry, he brought to it great talent, great industry and single-minded devotion. His sermons have all the qualities of his poems—massive learning, literary craftsmanship, swift and subtle reasoning, quaint but powerful imagery, intense feeling, the organ-toned music of his style wedded to the organ-toned music of his thought. It must have been something to hear him preach. It was preaching in the grand manner. But what chiefly impressed his hearers, as it impresses his readers today, was his almost overpowering earnestness. Preaching to him was not a rhetorical exercise. Like Richard Baxter, he preached "as a dying man to dying men."

One of his prose volumes is entitled *Devotions upon Emergent Occasions*. It is in the seventeenth of these (one wonders how he chanced upon it!) that Ernest Hemingway found the title of one of his finest novels: "No man is an Iland, intire of it selfe; every man is a peece of the Continent, a part of the Maine; if a Clod bee washed away by the Sea, Europe is the lesse . . . ; Any man's death diminishes me, because I am involved in Mankinde; And therefore never send to know for whom the bell tolls; It tolls for thee."

This is English prose in the great tradition of the *Areopagitica* and *Pilgrim's Progress* and Burke's "On Conciliation with the Colonies" and the Gettysburg Address. It is also great religion. The Bible from cover to cover insists on the solidarity of mankind; that no man lives unto himself—we are members one of another; that one is our Father and all we are brethren, sprung from a common source, involved in a common destiny, bound together in one bundle of life.

An isolated man is only half a man. What we are we are because of our relationships. It is these which give our lives meaning, dignity, worth. Only through others can we realize ourselves, express ourselves. A teacher cannot be a teacher alone; he becomes a teacher only when students come to him to be taught. A merchant cannot be a merchant alone; he becomes a merchant only as there are those from whom he can buy and those to whom he can sell. A doctor cannot be a doctor alone; he becomes a doctor only when patients come to him to be healed. A preacher becomes a preacher only when he has a congregation to preach to. So utterly dependent are we on others for the fulfillment of ourselves.

If this is true of these casual and professional relationships, how much more of life's central and mystical relationships: husband and wife, parent and child, lover and beloved, friend and friend. "No man is an Iland, intire of it selfe; every man is a peece of the Continent, a part of the Maine." That is the religious interpretation of this strange human life of ours. If we reject it, there is no other, and human life is a transient and insignificant episode on a whirling island in the sky.

There are many bitter things to be said about human nature, and at one time or another I have said most of them. But there is this to be said for human nature: generally speaking, the closer we come to people the more we like them, the more we recognize our kinship to them.

A story comes from the Arabic of a man who, looking out across the desert, saw an object on the horizon. He supposed it was a wild beast and prepared to run. As it came nearer he saw it was not a wild beast: it was a man on a camel. He supposed the man belonged to a hostile tribe and prepared to kill him. As the man came closer he saw he was not a member of a hostile tribe: he was a member of his own tribe. As he came still closer he saw it was his brother. That is a parable.

There was a time when I thought I did not like Welshmen —why I do not know, unless because of a nursery rhyme beginning, "Taffy was a Welshman, Taffy was a thief." Then I sat under a teacher who did for me more than any teacher I ever had. He was a Welshman to the core. He had a Welsh inscription carved over his fireplace; he was full of Welsh stories and songs, steeped in the lore of his native Wales. He was a luminous teacher, a man of complete intellectual honesty and the most sensitive conscience.

When I think of Englishmen in the mass, I resent their condescending, supercilious attitude toward lesser breeds without the law, including Americans. But the few English people I have known at all well have not been that way. A friend whose business takes him to England says the English always have time for the little courtesies, the little amenities; they don't push one another around as much as we do.

Twice in my lifetime the Germans have been our foes. But I grew up in a community with a large German element. Many of the boys I played with were of German extraction. I liked them. I like them still.

Italy played an inglorious role in both world wars. Mr. Roosevelt called it a jackal. Mr. Churchill—never to be outdone in epithets—called it a jackanapes. I shared their indignation, though I do not think anything is achieved by name-calling. But the Italians I know best are gardeners. They love the soil, they love to make things grow, they are the best and merriest-hearted gardeners in the world.

We fought a cruel war with Japan—cruel on both sides. But when during the war I asked a man who was born and brought up in Japan, "Did you like your Japanese friends as much as your friends here?" he replied, "Better." Said a missionary, returning to Japan after a furlough, "I'll be glad to get back to a place where the people's houses and lives are less cluttered than here and I can enjoy some good conversation."

One of the most encouraging things to be said about human nature, I repeat, is this: ordinarily, the closer we come to a man the more we like him, the more we feel our kinship to him. At a distance he looks like a beast, but when we get close enough we recognize a brother.

We belong to one another. We were made for one another. To the aristocratic Athenians Paul declared that God had "made of one blood every nation of men to dwell on all the face of the earth."

The biologist asserts that Paul's statement is scientifically correct. The brotherhood of man is not a sentimental phrase; it is a biological fact. Physically we are all cut from the same piece. One third of God's children are white, a little over a third black, a little less than a third yellow. But the human body makes the same response to heat, cold, food, pain, disease, whether it be garbed in black, white or yellow skin. Modern medicine accepts this as an axiom. The treatment of tuberculosis is the same for all. Insulin and quinine are everywhere equally efficacious. Cancer is no respecter of color or race. When people speak of different kinds of flesh and blood, they speak of what doesn't exist. There is but one kind of flesh among men—human flesh; but one kind of blood—human blood.

Mentally the same kinship is evident. Our intellectual status depends on our native endowment plus our training, not on our nationality. Modern pedagogy proceeds on the brave assumption that all children are teachable. Differences in capacity exist but are not due primarily to race. We are sometimes chagrined at the way in which foreign students, struggling against the disadvantage of an acquired language, strange customs and an unfamiliar environment, walk away with scholarships and prizes. Such experiences give a jolt to the myth of a "master race."

Anthropologists tell us that while there are superior individuals in every race, there is no evidence of marked superiority of one race over another. No race has a monopoly on virtue or on genius. Each has its distinctive contribution to make. Wherever one race touches another, each may learn and share and serve. No race is "an Iland, intire of it selfe; every race is a peece of the Continent, a part of the Maine." We do not have to decide whether we shall be brethren. God decided that when he made us of one blood. The question for us to decide is whether we shall be brotherly.

The great souls have always perceived their oneness with their kind. Said the old Roman sage: "I am a man; therefore I think that nothing human is foreign to me."

Said Gene Debs, released from the federal prison at Atlanta where he had been confined for his convictions against war: "As long as any man is in prison, I am in prison; as long as any man is in chains, I am not free."

Rabindranath Tagore was one of the eminent poets and noblest souls of our time. All his writings and all his life were motivated by love of God and love of humanity. His faith in one God of love impelled him to devote his life to working for one community of mankind. When after the first World War hundreds of Indians were massacred at Amritsar, Tagore fell into deep depression and returned the knighthood which had been given him. Yet at that very time he wrote to a friend: "I feel as much for the Negroes and for the Koreans as for the wrongs done to the helpless people of my own land."

So the great souls speak. The trouble with the rest of us is not that we're snobbish or hardhearted. We're deficient in imagination. We're absorbed in ourselves. We know that in our cities families live in rabbit warrens and hovels unfit for human habitation, children grow up in conditions corruptive of health and of decency. Whenever we drive through a blighted area we feel regret that people are obliged to live in such a drab environment. We give to the Community Chest in the hope that through its agencies their lives may be brightened. But with our bridge games and our golf games and our children's dancing class to attend to, we seldom give them a thought.

We haven't enough imagination to realize the literal truth of Theodore Roosevelt's assertion that no city is a good place for any of its people until it becomes a good place for all its people. Put it on the lowest, most selfish ground: as long as there are sore spots in a city, they endanger our health and safety. As long as there are a high tubercular rate and a high venereal rate among any element in the city's population they menace us and our children. And from a higher point of view, these people's lives are linked with ours. If we believe the New Testament is right in declaring Christ died for us, we must believe it is right in declaring Christ died for them.

We read of defenseless cities being bombed, we see pictures of hopeless people with the possessions they have rescued in bags on their heads or backs, dumb misery in their eyes, and it appalls us—we don't dare think too much about it or we'd go mad. But for the most part it rolls off us like water off a duck's back. It's all so far away, remote from the little orbit in which we move. We don't know any of these people. It seems unreal to us, like a pageant or shadow show, a motion picture which we watch flicker across the screen, then get up and walk out of the theater, blink our eyes and are back in our own cozy little world. If we looked at the world through the eyes of Christ, we should see in every one of these homeless folk a brother for whom Christ died, a man as dear to God as we are.

We are members one of another. Such is the teaching of the Bible from beginning to end. On almost its first page this note is struck. Two men stand face to face. One is a farmer, the other a sheep raiser. They are not competitors. Each is necessary to the other, one providing food, the other clothes. Their natural relationship is that of brothers. Their unnatural relationship is that of foes. Co-operation is their normal relation. The envy and malice which destroy it are abnormal. In a jealous rage one kills the other. Then, in the naïve anthropomorphism of the ancient narrative, we are told that God asked the murderer, "Where is your brother?" He answered, "Am I my brother's keeper?" And God said, "What have you done? The voice of your brother's blood is crying to me from the ground." It was not a matter of Cain and Abel only. It was Cain and Abel and God.

Brotherhood, not the denial of it, is man's primitive, instinctive reaction to his fellow. Watch a little child: he loves everyone, trusts everyone, shares with everyone, believes everyone is his friend, cannot understand why anyone should want to harm him. A few days ago I was standing on the curb when a small boy came up, slipped his hand in mine. When the light changed, he gripped my hand more tightly. We crossed the street together, then went our separate ways. An unspoiled child, surrounded by an atmosphere of love from the day he was born, he assumed I was a friendly person and would protect him. That is the natural, instinctive attitude. The attitude of aloofness, of indifference, of suspicion, of hostility, is unnatural.

We are our brother's keeper. We are made for one another. We belong to one another. We who are many are one body. According to the Bible we are bound together in a common sinfulness: "In Adam's fall we sinned all." There is a warp, a twist, an impediment in human nature which we all share. According to the Bible also we are bound together in a common redemption: "Christ died for all, wherefore henceforth we know no man after the flesh."

The truest interpreter Christ ever had saw in his cross the breaking down of walls of partition. These walls looked as solid in Paul's day as in ours—walls dividing race from race and man from man. But at Calvary something happened that knocked the props from under these walls: "God was in Christ reconciling the world to himself." "There cannot be Greek and Jew, barbarian, Scythian, slave or free, but Christ is all and in all. . . ." "In him all things hold together."

In Him shall true hearts everywhere
  Their high communion find;
His service is the golden cord
  Close binding all mankind.

Can we truly say that because Christ died for all we know no man after the flesh? Have we allowed his cross to blot out for us the distinctions which estrange? Do we know and feel that, because one is our Father, beneath all our differences beats one common heart of mankind?

Look out across the world. Never were we so close together.

Never were we so far apart. The things that bind us together are obscured. The things that set us at odds are magnified. In face of the world's blatant denial of man's brotherhood, God help us to affirm it and to live it:

> O brother man, fold to thy heart thy brother;
> Where pity dwells, the peace of God is there;
> To worship rightly is to love each other,
> Each smile a hymn, each kindly deed a prayer.

"No man is an Iland, intire of it selfe; every man is a peece of the Continent, a part of the Maine; . . . Any man's death diminishes me, because I am involved in Mankinde; And therefore never send to know for whom the bell tolls; It tolls for thee."

✠

Prayer

MAY THE BLESSING of God rest upon all his people in every land, of every tongue. The Lord meet in mercy all who seek him by whatever name or sign. The Lord comfort all who suffer and mourn both near and far away. The Lord bless us and keep us and grant us his peace. Amen.

V

The Three Distances

In a lecture on "The Making of the Novel," Hugh Walpole declared that the novelist must have conviction, sincerity and vision. Of the last requisite he said:

> The novelist must have what I would call a sense of the Three Distances. When we walk in the country we are aware of three ranges of vision. Close beside us is the immediate scene, the carter driving past us up the hill, the child picking flowers in the hedge; at the next range we are aware of the details of the fields about us, the grass, the trees, the gently climbing hill; and then beyond these there is the open country, the hills a faint line against the sky, the great sweeping arc checkered with cloud and color uniting us with other worlds that are far beyond our limited vision.
>
> Every novel that fulfills its true purpose must have these Three Distances: (1) immediate action, movements, personalities of a few characters close to us; then (2) the background of this earthly life fitting around them in its beautiful detail; then (3) beyond these a wider, all-enveloping vision, a philosophy that, however faulty and inadequate, tries to give some meaning to this strange earthly existence.

I go a step farther and say that a life which fulfills its true purpose, no less than the novel which seeks to portray life, must have these three distances: the near view, the wide view, the far view; must see each in its true perspective and its relation to the other two.

Link with Hugh Walpole's statement a sentence from Isaiah (33:17): "Your eyes will see the king in his beauty . . . and a land that stretches afar."

There is beauty and meaning in the near view, the life about us, our familiar relations, our commonplace tasks. True for us as for Moses, "The place on which you stand is holy ground." Once a friend, returned from a pilgrimage to Palestine, offered me a bottle of water from the Jordan River to use in baptisms. I assured him that to me Lake Erie water is just as sacramental as water brought from the Holy Land.

If myopia, the inability to see things at a distance, is a spiritual no less than a physical infirmity, equally so is its opposite, the inability to see and appreciate things right at hand. Pity the man who has become so exalted he can no longer see the sacramental meaning of the passing day, the routine duty well done, the little courtesy, the cheerful greeting, the mealtimes, the dear ties which bind us to one another and are the divinest thing this fugitive life can show.

A reformer once remarked to Julia Ward Howe that he was interested in principles and programs for social betterment but had ceased to be interested in individuals. Mrs. Howe replied that she was glad God had not reached that point.

Especially at Christmas when life is seen in the radiance that streamed from Bethlehem's star, we realize how much our own little circle means to us. How appealing our children are! Even the neighbors' children seem strangely attractive, as we see all childhood in the light that came into the world with Mary's child. How good our friends seem! How we cherish them and thank God for them!

My house, like yours, is full of Christmas cards. There are cards from people I see right along in my work; cards from some I rarely see; cards from people I united in marriage or whose children I baptized or beside whose dead I stood to speak the words our faith, hope and love prompt; cards from friends of student days, who never write me through the year because they are preoccupied with their work as I am with mine, but how good it is to learn that they have not forgotten. The older we grow the surer we are that the finest thing in life is friendship, a thing so good it more than compensates for all life's pain and loss.

Even our work, which at times seems a grim tyrant, how good it is! To know that we are able to pay our way through the world, that others rely on us for some needed contribution to the common weal: this is one of life's durable satisfactions. At Christmas we see it as something more than the means by which we get our living. We see those who are associated with us in it not as cogs in a machine but as human beings with human interests and affections like our own.

There is beauty and meaning in the near view, have we the wit to perceive it. Only when we see nothing beyond it does it seem petty and insignificant. It is as we see it against a wider background, our little life against the horizon of the world's life, our little part in the light of the whole, that its meaning and beauty become plain.

So we must not restrict our vision to the near view if we would make our lives symmetrical and beautiful. I do not use the adjective *beautiful* in any vague sense, but as Aristotle used it, who said that "the essence of the beautiful consists in amplitude and order"—seeing things in their fullness and in their right relations, if I may venture to paraphrase.

Christians in our day are cultivating the wide view as never before. In the light of the tragic events which will make the first half of the twentieth century forever memorable and forever terrible in the eyes of posterity, we have learned that it is not enough to cultivate beautiful dispositions in ourselves and our children; we must make the principles of Jesus and the spirit of Jesus prevail in the world he came to save. This is not a pious sentiment; it is the alternative to destruction. No generation has prayed more wistfully, more earnestly than ours, "Thy kingdom come, thy will be done on earth."

Not to weary you with a survey of the historical situation in Isaiah's day, let me simply say that it was during the siege of Jerusalem by the Assyrians under Sennacherib in the days of good King Hezekiah. During the siege Hezekiah covered himself with sackcloth and ashes and humbled himself before God. He was also disfigured by boils, probably the result of the malnutrition and unsanitary conditions incident to a long siege. Isaiah promised deliverance from this trying situation: "Your eyes will see the king in his beauty"—no longer covered with boils and sackcloth, but restored to health and clothed in his robes of state—"and a land that stretches afar"—no longer will their vision be confined to the narrow streets and closed gates of Jerusalem, they will be able to go out into the countryside and feast their eyes on sweeping landscapes and wide horizons. We can imagine how delightful that prospect would be to people long imprisoned in a beleaguered city. This is the primary meaning of Isaiah's prophecy.

It may have a Messianic meaning also. "The king in his beauty" may refer to the long-awaited Messiah and "the land that stretches afar" to the all-embracing kingdom of God which his coming would usher in. Isaiah's life was restricted by the most narrowing and thwarting circumstances, but he was able to cherish the wide outlook that sets the spirit free.

So it was with the man who wrote the book of visions with which the Bible ends. He was an exile, cooped up on Patmos, a tiny island in the eastern Mediterranean, so small one can scarcely find it on the map. Yet one needs only to read the Revelation to see that all the important political and religious movements of his time swept through his mind.

I think it is especially true of life in a big city that the foreground looms so large it tends to smother the background—of cloud and horizon, of spacious thought and quiet meditation. We are imprisoned in the office, the shop, the schoolroom, the home, wherever our work is done. So many people to be seen, so many letters to be written, so many phone calls to be made, so many orders to be filled, so many things to be done, then done again: such is our daily routine and some of us seldom see beyond it. Our lives are like Dick Swiveller's room, of which he told the little old gentleman to whom he was trying to lease it that it afforded "an uninterrupted view across the street."

Perhaps you feel that your life is thwarted by limitations you cannot remove, cramped by circumstances you cannot control; but so long as you have any power of imagination, you—like Isaiah and John—can make your own world and live in it. For a man's life is as large as his vision and no larger. I love these oft-quoted lines of Edna St. Vincent Millay:

The world stands out on either side
No wider than the heart is wide;
Above the world is stretched the sky,
No higher than the soul is high.
The heart can push the sea and land
Farther away on either hand;
The soul can split the sky in two
And let the face of God shine through.
But East and West will pinch the heart
That cannot keep them pushed apart;
And he whose soul is flat, the sky
Will cave in on him by and by.

There are beauty and meaning in the near view, there are beauty and meaning in the wide view, but we never fully appreciate either until we see them in relation to the third distance of which Hugh Walpole speaks—the far view, a view which runs on beyond the rim of this world.

At the transit of the years we are most conscious of the passage of time, of how fleeting is our tenure here. Do you ever think of the mystery of time, ask yourself what it is? It seems to be related to another mystery—space. Astronomers use time to measure space. Interstellar distances are too vast to be measured by the yardstick or the mile, so they use as their unit of measurement the light-year, that is, the distance it takes a ray of light, traveling 186,000 miles per second, a year to traverse—in round numbers, 6,000,000,000,000 miles. The nearest star to us, Alpha Centauri, is four and one-third light-years away. Sirius, the dog star, twenty-eight times as bright as the sun, is between eight and nine light-years away. There are only three stars less than ten light-years from us. Arcturus, 100 times as bright as the sun, is thirty-three light-years from us; Rigel, 10,000 times as bright as the sun, is 500 light-years from us.

Long ago a man looked up into the Syrian sky and asked, "Can you bind the chains of the Pleiades, or loose the cords of Orion?" (Job 38:31.) The answer becomes apparent when we reflect that the Pleiades are a cluster of 300 to 500 stars, thirty light-years in diameter, 325 light-years from us, and that Orion, the giant hunter with his girdle, is a group of blue stars 600 light-years away. Both would seem quite safe from human intrusion. Now we are getting into "the land of far distances," but only a little way.

One night an astronomer pointed out to me the cluster of Hercules. You can see it with the naked eye and no wonder, for it contains 35,000 stars as bright as the sun, some a hundred times as bright; the diameter of the cluster is 350 light-years and it is 36,000 light-years away. The light we see when we look at it started toward us 36,000 years ago. When we recall that civilization dawned on this planet in the Nile and Tigris-Euphrates valleys only about 6,000 years ago, we realize what Sir William Herschel meant when he said that the telescope penetrates into time as well as into space. We appreciate his remark to his nervous brother, who was inclined to be easily panic-striken, "Think of the star clusters"—the inference being that the Power that controls the star clusters can control our little lives.

When we get beyond the cluster of Hercules, we feel a long way from home; yet it is one of the nearest of the star clusters. Another is 230,000 light-years away. Our galaxy is 300,000 light-years in diameter. Our Milky Way is a collection of billions of stars. It is borne in upon us that no man-made disturbance on the surface of this little planet, however serious and distressing to him, is likely to throw the universe out of gear.

Beyond our system lie other galaxies, like the large Magellanic cloud, which contains 200,000 giant suns, each more than 150 times as bright as our sun; 2,000 of them are 10,000 times as bright as our sun, some are 100,000 times brighter. The large Magellanic cloud is 50,000,000 light-years from us. There are other galaxies and spiral nebulae 170,000,000 light-years from us. And beyond that? Is space infinite or does it have an end?—a purely academic question.

You see how time and space run into each other. If you could annihilate space, you would annihilate time. The word *infinity* has reference to space, the word *eternity* has reference to time. When we speak of the infinite and eternal God, we use no empty phrase. If we can conceive of a Being who is not only transcendent over his creation but immanent in it—that is, if we can conceive of the omnipresence of God—then there is no near and far, no past and future to him. Time and space have no meaning to him. He is "the high and lofty One who inhabits eternity," living in one grand inclusive now.

Yet this material creation with its unimaginable distances, its unrecorded millennia of time, seems to resolve into and emanate from another which is immaterial and invisible. It used to be said that the unit of matter was the atom. Lucretius in his *De Rerum Natura* (first century B.C.) lists the characteristics of the atom: it is immutable, indestructible, indivisible, it cannot be resolved into anything smaller or more basic than itself.

Today we know that the atom is a universe in itself. The physicist resolves it into electrons, bits of negative electricity revolving around a nucleus of positive electricity. The electron is not matter, in the common use of the word. You cannot see or touch or weigh it; yet it is the basis of the material universe—a strain in the ether, a tension of the ether, a motion of the ether, a property of the ether. But if it is not matter, what is it—spirit?

So eminent a scientist as J. B. S. Haldane goes so far as to assert that "the material world is only the spiritual world imperfectly and partially perceived"—a statement with which I believe Plato, greatest of idealistic philosophers, would agree. Can it be that this all-embracing ether which penetrates and clasps and holds the world is closely related to, if not identical with, the will of God?

So by this long approach we come to the portals of the spiritual world, the real world, of which we are citizens now and evermore. God is spirit. We are spirits, too. Just as God inhabits this physical universe, expresses himself through it but is something other and more than the physical universe, so we inhabit these physical bodies, express ourselves through them but are something other and more than they. Your body is not the real you. It is only your garment, continually woven and rewoven for you out of chemical substances in the blood. The body you have today is no more the body you had seven years ago than the fire in your furnace this morning is the fire that was there last night. My hand is not the hand I had seven years ago: not a cell of that hand remains. The brain with which I think now is not the brain with which I thought seven years ago: not one cell of that brain is left. Yet in my thought life there is an unbroken continuity, so that I can remember and utilize things I learned twenty, thirty, forty years ago. As I consider how I have survived the death of every part of my body time and time again, I find it easier to believe I shall survive the final death of my body when it returns to the dust from which it came.

No, I cannot prove it, but it is the anticipation which every analogy from the physical world suggests and confirms. The poet speaks of death as "a leap into the dark." It may prove less of a leap and far less dark than we suppose—just a closing of the eyes here and an opening of them there. May not our birth into the world to which we go be as natural as our birth into this? May not our terror at the thought of it be as baseless as that of Don Quixote when blindfolded he hangs by his wrist from the stable window and is told that a bottomless abyss yawns beneath him? The gallant gentleman is palsied with fear. When Maritornes, laughing to himself, cuts the thong, he falls—just four inches. May there not be as blithesome a surprise in store for us when our time comes to discover the nearness of the unseen world? And just as when we entered this world a stranger, helpless, tiny, "with no language but a cry," we found loving presences awaiting us who supplied our every need, may it be that when we pass through the portals of death we shall find not a lonely but a friendly place, where loving presences wait to welcome us—above all, One who went before us to prepare the way, that where he is there we may also be?

"God forgive me if I am wrong," said Charles Kingsley of his approaching death, "but I look forward to it with an intense and reverent curiosity." So it seemed to Thomas Carlyle: "Eternity, which cannot be far off now, is my one strong city. I look into it fixedly now and then. All terrors about it seem superfluous."

So it seemed to the old Christian who wrote the thrilling triumph song with which the Bible ends. What a fair face it wore to him! What a friendly face! What a human face! He calls it Christ, and it is the voice of Christ he records in style and language of his own:

> I am the Alpha and the Omega,
> The first one and likewise the last one,
> The beginning and also the ending.
> The Spirit and the Bride say, "Come."
> And let him who hears say, "Come."
> He that is athirst, let him come.
> Yes, whoever will,
> Let him take the water of life freely.

✠

Prayer

ANCIENT OF DAYS, who continuest when earth and heaven wax old like a garment, take the veil from our eyes that in the quiet of this holy hour we may see thee. How deeply we are immersed in time, in the things that wax and wane and pass away! How little we enjoy the power of eternal life, which even now is ours. Teach us to turn the stuff of this life into the material of eternity.

Show us the way through the things that are seen and transient to the things that are unseen and eternal. Enable us to taste the power of the age to come, lest this present world gain dominion over us. Make plain to us that the incidents of our fugitive days are of little moment and quickly gone, but the courage, the faith, the generosity they call forth are of surpassing worth, a part of the self that lives forever because it is akin to thee. So may all our experiences, our failures as well as our victories, the bitter as well as the sweet, be steppingstones along the straight way that leads to eternal life.

It may be that in this new year we shall be called upon to wrestle with the mystery of suffering or temptation or death. Maybe we shall catch some new vision of thee, see the King in his beauty and the land that stretches afar. Maybe there will come some great chance to bear witness for Christ, to serve and bless one of our brothers for whom Christ died. This may be the year for which all our years have prepared the way. May we not be found drowsy in the day of our visitation but alert and eager, strong and brave. And whether the call be to face peril or loss or to give help where help is needed, enable us to meet it with a high heart and an obedient will.

So may we enter the new year joyously, expectantly, sure that the future like the past belongs to thee; thankful that in this transient world we are able to lay up treasure where neither moth nor rust can consume nor thieves break through and steal; confident that whatever the muffled days bring us the eternal God is our dwelling place and underneath are the everlasting arms, that as our days so shall our strength be, that thou wilt keep him in perfect peace whose mind is stayed on thee. Amen.

VI

Standing Up to Life

THE MOST difficult of personal problems as life advances is that of keeping up one's morale. This is not the orthodox opinion. The orthodox opinion, as you may learn from dipping into the flood of books on popular psychology, psychiatry and psychoanalysis, is that our chief personal problem is the control of the instincts. That is a problem. But without minimizing its difficulty or importance, I speak to the experience of many when I say that one of the rewards of a well-spent life, a life filled with wholesome interests and steered by wholesome purposes, is that our instincts become progressively easier to handle aright. Not by asceticism but by a reasonable self-discipline we can convert them from accomplices to allies. But again I speak to the experience of many when I say that the problem of keeping up one's morale does not grow easier as we fare along. Often it grows harder.

Forgive a personal testimony. You recall how Emerson, when he had diffidently let slip some secret of his soul, supposing it peculiar to him, was amazed to discover that others had had the same experience. They would write to tell him he had put his finger on their case exactly, though they had never put it into words.

I sometimes seem to myself to be leading a double life—not in the opprobrious sense. My outer life consists largely of routine duties and the ordinary human relationships. Behind this is my inner life—the things I think about and dream about. It has points of contact with my outer life but I have never quite harmonized the two. Perhaps it is not necessary nor desirable that one should. But here is the point: as I grow older I find that my outer life, my struggle with the world, on the whole becomes easier, but that my inner life, my struggle with myself, becomes no less hard.

The early years of my ministry were trying. I used up a good deal of nervous energy. I breathed a sigh of relief when each Sunday was over. I was so timid and self-distrustful in dealing with individuals who had moral or personal problems that, if I had a difficult interview before me, I worried about it till it came and was ill at ease till it was over. No doubt men in other kinds of work have similar experiences. I have often tried to imagine how a doctor feels when his first patient knocks at his office door or when he enters the operating room to perform his first operation or deliver his first baby; how the teacher feels when for the first time she stands before her class and realizes how slight is her own mental superiority. With time and practice come the mastery of the technique of one's work and some consciousness of personal power. The doctor acquires a brisk, confident, professional air. The teacher lays down the law as though all wisdom began and ended in her. The preacher becomes almost too facile, glib, self-assured. But while we thus learn how better to handle the externals of life, our inner problems remain. They may change but they do not become easier. The need for self-discipline is unabated to the end. Not less but more do we feel the need of the courage, the endurance, the poise that enable us to stand up to life.

The Bible, which anticipates our every experience, our every inner need, has much to say about this. One of the great words of the New Testament is "endure." "He who endures to the end will be saved," it reports Jesus to have said. "Consider him"—him, that is, who "endured the cross, despising the shame"—"so that you may not grow weary or faint-hearted. . . . You have not yet resisted to the point of shedding blood," says the Letter to the Hebrews, which also holds up for our example Moses, who "endured, as seeing him who is invisible."

"Endure hardship as a good soldier," writes Paul. In the bracing passage where he pictures the Christian life as a warfare, the recurrent word is "stand": "Put on the whole armor of God, that you may be able to stand against the wiles of the devil. For we are not contending against flesh and blood, but against the principalities, against the powers, against the world rulers of this present darkness, against the spiritual hosts of wickedness in the heavenly places. Therefore take the whole armor of God, that you may be able to withstand in the evil day, and having done all, to stand."

The Bible nowhere leads us to expect that life is easy or will grow easier. We might go so far as to say that the main teaching of the Bible, the teaching on which it is most insistent save for one other, is that in this world we shall never be free of difficulties, that it is struggle, struggle, struggle all the way. The supreme doctrine of the Bible, to which this other is subsidiary, is that we are not alone, that we have resources to draw upon and an unfaltering Ally. These two doctrines constitute in briefest compass the religious interpretation of life. They are complementary, like light and shade. They stand or fall together, so that when the souls of men fall away from the one, they fall away also from the other.

Indeed, it is the idea of God which in a way creates our difficulty. When we suffer it is nearly always for our faith; and deep observers of the soul, like Augustine, Bunyan, Paul and the author of the Seventy-third Psalm, confess that again and again their souls have been such a battleground that they have envied the beasts of the field which have no sense of God and are therefore exempt from man's ever-failing, never-ending struggle to achieve the godlike in his own life.

It ought frankly to be conceded that the coming of Christ has not made life easier. For he has set before us a standard of behaviour higher and more difficult of attainment than the most enlightened men before his time had even imagined. A single illustration: the Greek historian, Xenophon, who was a favorite disciple of Socrates, in his *Cyropedia* climaxes his praise of his hero, Cyrus the Younger, by asserting that no man ever did more good to his friends or more harm to his foes. That was good Greek morality and the Greeks were the most civilized people on earth. I can live up to that. Just by following my natural inclinations I can live up to that. I like to do nice things for my friends. I like to play tit for tat with those who have done mean things to me. But when I turn to the Sermon on the Mount I read: "You have heard that it was said, 'An eye for an eye and a tooth for a tooth.' But I say to you, Do not resist one who is evil. But if any one strikes you on the right cheek, turn to him the other also. . . . You have heard that it was said, 'You shall love your neighbor and hate your enemy.' But I say to you, Love your enemies and pray for those who persecute you."

It is not easy for me to live up to that. I have to crucify my natural impulses to live up to that. No, the coming of Christ has made life harder by setting before us a standard of behavior which, once seen, makes us dissatisfied with any other and with ourselves, because we continually fall short of it.

Even more, the coming of Christ has made life difficult by widening and deepening the area of suffering. For the effect of any sincere relationship with Christ is to make us more sensitive. A sensitive man runs more risk of getting hurt than one who has allowed his skin to grow tough as the hide of a rhinoceros. All of us know rhinoceros men. They do not suffer in the sufferings of others. They do not suffer from their own sins, except when the consequence of their sins catches up with them. But the followers of Christ are not so: the first effect he has upon us is to make us more sensitive.

Some resent this, going so far as to say that Christ has taken the color out of life, cast a pall over men's spirits, made impossible the joyous, carefree abandon which we associate with the spirit of the Greek.

"Thou hast conquered, O pale Galilean," sings Swinburne. "The world has grown gray at thy breath!" One wonders where even poetic license could have found evidence that Christ was "pale" and that his influence makes life drab. According to the Fourth Gospel, he wrought his first "sign" at a wedding supper, and he wrought it that the party might go on. According to the earlier gospels, a charge brought against him by his foes was that he made friends with disreputable characters, seeking them out, apparently preferring their company to that of staid and ultrarespectable folk. He seems to have been a most unconventional person; and, arduous as his life was, it was not without romance. Nor is there anything "pale" about one who drove the money-changers from the temple and flung their furniture after them. No, if the effect of Christ on life has been to make it a wan and negative and frightened thing, this is far from the description he gave of his purpose in coming among us. He came, he said, that men might have life and have it abundantly.

Certainly in this forecast of his influence he was correct. For the book of the Acts, which describes the situation immediately after he had come and gone, gives the impression of an unforced and bubbling vitality. "They ate their food with gladness," we read of the disciples, "praising God." Every meal was a eucharist, a feast of thanksgiving. The hymns they sang were cheerful, even gay. Despite the shadow of the grim tragedy which brought their Master's life to a close, they were so merry they were suspected of being too convivial. On the Day of Pentecost they were so hilarious Peter had to defend them against the charge of being drunk! And with it all, their amazing success in establishing and extending the new faith. But the vitality they displayed was not a mere exuberance of animal spirits, like that of boys let out of school. It was the kind of vitality which dealt sternly with those who trifled with truth or purity or honor, as strong in its restraints as in its freedom.

It is true that people who are out to do what they like, who have no liking for self-discipline, let alone self-denial, find themselves embarrassed and rebuked when they come into the presence of Christ, feeling that by his presence their lives are judged. Whereupon they blame him for the loftiness of his standards and the elevation of his character instead of themselves for their slackness.

As a matter of fact, life has always been harder for some

than for others, not only because for some people things seem to go wrong all out of proportion to their deserts but because some expect of themselves finer things which do not come easily or naturally. Life is one thing for those who are rowing upstream and another for those who drift with the tide.

Admiral Byrd says that during his first winter in the Antarctic he asked an Irishman in his ship's company what he missed most of civilization. He answered, "Temptation." I suspect there was more in the reply than Irish wit: the recognition that it is in temptation that the power of the will—that power which differentiates man from the brute—has its best chance to assert itself. It is temptation that makes or breaks a man, according as he stands up to it, defies it, triumphs over it, or succumbs to it and acquiesces in it.

We do well to vary our method in dealing with temptation. Sometimes the best strategy is a spirited attack; other times, a swift retreat. Washington is acclaimed a first-rank military genius, yet his campaigns in our War of Independence consisted largely of a series of masterly retreats. He never won a major battle, but he won the war.

Homer tells a story of the much-traveled Odysseus, which he rightly supposes we shall put to his credit. Knowing what was coming and what manner of man he was, Odysseus, as he approached the sirens' isle, gathered his crew about him and talked to them seriously. The substance of what he said was that they were approaching the home of the sirens and that if he were left to himself he should go ashore and go to pieces. Therefore, while he was still at a distance and master of himself, he bade them take it as his final order that they were not to land there. They were not even to cast anchor outside. They were to crowd the canvas and sail on. Undoubtedly he would want to land when the sirens came into view and their seductive music filled his ears. That was why he had called them together now.

They were to tie him to the mast as though he were mad. He would be mad when he heard the sirens' song. The more he pleaded to be let free, the tauter they were to draw the ropes. If he howled like a dog and foamed at the mouth, cursing their interference, they were to pay no heed. At that stage it might be easier for them if they poured wax in his ears and their own. Thus was the much-traveled Odysseus able to return home to Penelope, who was faithfully awaiting him. And there was that about his returning countenance, we are told, which caused her suitors to stand not on the order of their going. In Homer's view of life and of the difficult business of getting through it with one's soul intact, there was nothing to be ashamed of in that story.

Life, I repeat, is one thing for those who resist temptation and another for those who never stand up to it at all. It is only those who fight against their appetites and the tyranny of old, bad habits who know their awful power. Those who yield to them think they are nothing. But it is as we tug against the forces which would drag us downward that the sinews of the soul grow strong.

And the direction which the world in any age will take depends on the preponderance of those who are pulling upstream over those who are drifting with the tide or vice versa. If the idealists have never yet gained the mastery, at least they have never yet been driven from the field. They come back again and again after what looks like utter rout. It would seem that there is something in the nature of things that in the long run works against a self-indulgent way of life.

We have with us today, we have always had with us, the cult of naturalism, whose most inspired motto is "Express your instincts, obey your impulses, gratify your desires, repression is dangerous." But man at his best has always lived by an other-than-natural law. The essence of culture is self-restraint, the will triumphing over the natural impulses and inclinations. Call it dissembling if you like, but the man who puts on the cloak of good humor when his nerves are on edge, who speaks the generous word of praise when he is tortured by jealousy, who resolutely holds himself to the truth when it is to his immediate advantage to lie, who refuses to inflict on others the variability of his own moods, is the gentleman. A gentleman is careful to consume his own smoke, not to pollute the atmosphere others must breathe.

The good life, it should frankly be said, is not a native endowment, like curly hair or an ear for music. It is an achievement. In a sense, it is unnatural, just as walking is unnatural, consisting as it does in starting to fall and catching oneself, starting to fall and catching oneself again. Walking is not a native endowment. It is something man, whose ancestors were quadrupeds, has had to learn with many a bump and many a fall and which every new generation has to learn for itself. The good life is even so. In a sense it is something we "put on," as Paul bids us "put on the whole armor of God."

It is folly to call a man a hypocrite because when he feels like knocking his neighbor down he smiles and shakes hands with him instead. The woman who greets her guests graciously, tells them it was good of them to come, when she is so tired she can hardly stand, exhibits genuine self-mastery. The businessman who is overpunctilious about money matters because he is aware of a dishonest or an avaricious streak in his make-up is as heroic as the congenital coward who forces himself to deeds of valor. A beautiful character is like a beautiful picture: it is the product of long-continued training, effort, skill. The good life is no more a natural thing than is the ability to speak the English language with precision and grace. The hardest thing in the world, the finest of all the fine arts, is to live an ordinary life well.

Sometimes, as I have hinted, it grows harder as we grow older. When a crisis comes we usually rise to meet it. But how do we react to the petty annoyances of life or the incidental failure which comes to everyone, for not even the most fortunate are uniformly successful? The resilience of youth takes such things easily—when knocked down, gets up again—but we older folk, instead of taking them philosophically and allowing them to teach us patience, perseverance, self-control, often allow ourselves to be pushed down into petulance or cynicism or bitterness or hardness or envy or self-pity. Nor does the mere passage of time solve the problems of the inner life; they have to be stood up to and wrestled with with the rough hands of a man desperately in earnest. But so long as a man keeps struggling, no matter how often defeated, there is hope for him. And the hope of the world lies in those who keep up the good fight.

The Bible is always prepared for the worst. It never conceals from itself that a time may come when only a remnant will remain who will hold the race to finer things. But the Bible is sure God never leaves himself without a witness. It stakes everything on the continuing presence in the world of men capable of holding themselves to the highest that they know.

And these will always be busy men, burdened men. We chafe, some of us, under our incessant duties. We ought rather to thank God for them. For Bishop Butler is right when he tells us that to dispose a man to holiness the active life is better than the contemplative life. It is when his hands and feet, his mind and heart are busy, when he has tasks which tax him to the uttermost, that a man is safest. In the most winsome of all his invitations to the sons of men, our Lord invites those who are weary and heavy laden to take on an added burden! For he knows that we behave better under a heavy load than under a light one.

But the Lord is full of compassion, and the Bible, which is the supreme record of the mind of God, is full of understanding. There are times, it confesses, when we "faint," when the way seems long and our spirits wilt beneath the heat of the noonday sun, when we may even question the worth of struggling on. The New Testament, as we have seen, bristles with warnings and specifics against this haunting disease of the soul, which Spenser in *The Faerie Queene* calls "accidie"—falling away—and Dante in *The Divine Comedy* describes as "a rotten sin."

To anyone who reads the New Testament and reads between the lines, asking himself why this word or appeal was used and not another, it is obvious that at the time it was written the church was in critical condition. Apart from the effect of persecution, which, though it separates the wheat from the chaff, never fails to damage the wheat, all the old appetites and weaknesses were reasserting themselves.

Certainly the New Testament's most frequent appeal is for Christians to stand their ground, to hold on. Indeed, many scholars believe it was to check the beginnings of an apostasy that Mark, our earliest gospel, was written. It was written in Rome. It is based on the reminiscences of Peter, who had suffered martyrdom there not long before. Mark wrote what is often called the "martyr gospel" to brace and rally the Roman Christians just emerging from one persecution and likely at any time to face another. It gives us not so much the story of Jesus' life as the story of his sufferings and his steadfast endurance of them. It gives the impression—does it not?—that it is hurrying to its close.

One third of its pages are taken up by the last week of Jesus' life. When at length the evangelist comes within sight of the cross, his pace slackens. He spares us nothing. He makes us stand and watch the stages of his dying, as though insisting that we who bear the name of Christ must not forget what he had to bear, as though summoning us to ask ourselves what we mean to do with those secret departures from an earlier loyalty which in the light of the cross make us ashamed.

One of the finest chapters in the Old Testament is the fortieth of Isaiah. Its finest sentence is its last. The finest thing about that last sentence is its climax. At first it seems like an anticlimax, but it is not. "Even youths shall faint and be weary, and young men shall fall exhausted; but they who wait upon the Lord shall renew their strength, they shall mount up with wings like eagles, they shall run and not be weary, they shall walk and not faint."

It is exhilarating to mount up with wings as eagles. It is glorious to be able to run and not be weary. But the man God can use, the man who wins at the last the only crown worth striving for, is he who with a smile on his face through the weary years can walk and not faint. And who can say what his joy will be who, coming to the end of the hard-fought day scarred and spent but undishonored and undismayed, can look into his Lord's face and say, "I have fought the good fight, I have finished the course, I have kept the faith"? For he who endures to the end will be saved.

✠

Prayer

O God, thou knowest how sorely in these difficult days we need this tonic message of our faith. Some of us are tired. Some are disappointed. Some are discouraged and at our wit's end. Some must carry the burdens of others in addition to our own. All of us are hard bestead, tempted—it may be—to pull down the flag and slink like cowards from the field. Therefore have we come here this day, seeking something or Someone who can enable us to stand up to life and see it through.

O Christ, our captain in the well-fought fight, put new hope and courage into us. Brace us to play the man. Help us to endure, as seeing him who is invisible. Impel us to put on the whole armor of God that we may be able to withstand in the evil day and, having done all, to stand.

Unto thee, who art able to guard us from stumbling and to present us blameless before the presence of thy glory with exceeding joy, be glory, majesty, dominion and power, now and evermore. Amen.

VII

What Is Faith?

NO WORDS are harder to grasp than those which are familiar. This is especially true of a word like *faith,* which many regard as a word used in religious circles in a mysterious and esoteric sense. *Faith* is one of the great words of religion, and certain associations and a certain emotional content have attached themselves to it through the years, as when we sing, "My faith looks up to thee" or "Faith of our fathers, living still." But bear in mind that *faith* as used in religion means basically what it means in common speech. If I say, "I have faith in you," you know what I mean; if I say, "I have no faith in you," you know what I mean. I don't need to define it.

Emerson thought that when a word became threadbare or a cant word it was time to discard it and get a new one. He thought that fate had befallen the word *God,* that it slipped through people's minds without leaving a dent, so he began to speak of the *Oversoul* instead. I have sometimes thought that *faith* has become a cant word, that we might do well to substitute another word for it, say *confidence.* But why use a three-syllable word when a monosyllable will do? Besides, when you look at the word *confidence* you see that its root is *fides,* the Latin word for *faith.* Better to keep the old word and put new life into it.

Faith is one of the great words of the New Testament. It is found only once in the Old Testament, the famous sentence in Habakkuk, "The righteous shall live by his faith," which Paul seized on and made the basis of the doctrine we always associate with his name—Justification by Faith. In the New Testament it occurs almost 250 times, in twenty-four of the twenty-seven New Testament books.

It was a favorite word of Jesus. He was using it all the time. On the last Monday of his life he said to Peter, "Have faith in God." He had said the same thing before. He will go on saying it to the end. "Have faith in God."

Not only was he always speaking about faith; he was always looking for faith. He looked for it in his disciples, for he knew that without faith it was impossible for them to carry on his work. He never reproached them because they had no money or because they were not clever. He did reproach them for their lack of faith: "O men of little faith!"

One day their ship was caught in a storm. The wind blew furiously until it blew their faith away. "Have you no faith?" he asked them. He could not understand it. It seemed to him astonishing that men living in a world like this should have no faith.

He was not unreasonable. He did not expect them to have as much faith as he had, but he did expect a little. "If you have faith as a grain of mustard seed, you will say to this mountain, 'Move hence to yonder place,' and it will move; and nothing will be impossible to you." In other words, if you have as much faith as the smallest thing you know, you can say to the biggest thing you know, "Move," and it will move. Without faith nothing is possible. With faith nothing is impossible.

Faith is contagious. It cannot be taught but it can be caught. Jesus was so full of faith that his disciples caught it from him. When they had a little they wanted more. They began to say, "Lord, increase our faith!" As he watched their faith grow, Jesus rejoiced.

But faith is a treasure that can be lost. Jesus was concerned lest his disciples should lose theirs. One day he opened his heart to Peter: "Satan demanded to have you, that he might sift you like wheat, but I have prayed for you that your faith may not fail." He knew that if Peter's faith failed, it was all up with him.

If the absence of faith distressed Jesus, nothing so encouraged and exhilarated him as to discover it, especially in unexpected quarters. He found it one day in a Roman centurion. The Romans were not famed for their spirituality. But in the city of Capernaum Jesus found a centurion who drew from him these glowing words of praise: "Not even in Israel have I found such faith."

Once he was astonished in the same way by the faith of a woman, a foreign woman at that. "O woman, great is your faith!" he exclaimed. It was the highest eulogy he could pay. When men whom he had helped and healed were leaving him he often called after them, "Your faith did it! Your faith has made you well."

When from the gospels we pass to the letters of Paul, we find the word *faith* on every page—over a hundred times in the little sheaf of his correspondence which has come down to us. He could not put his pen into the ink bottle without bringing up on the point of it the word *faith*.

Let me remind you of two things he says about faith. In his letter to the Romans he writes: "I bid every one of you not to think of himself more highly than he ought to think, but to make a sober estimate of himself, according to the degree of faith God has given him."

That is, let every man estimate himself by the amount of faith he possesses. What a quaint idea! This is not how we estimate ourselves. We estimate ourselves by other standards: our money, our education, our business sagacity, our standing in the community, our cleverness, our intellectual acumen.

Whoever heard of a man estimating himself by his faith? No wonder those whom the world accounts successful are prone to think of themselves more highly than they ought to think! They are sure to do so when they measure themselves by their money or their talents, their intellectual prowess, their business or social prestige. It is not till we begin to measure ourselves by our faith that we become humble. Then we discover how poor we are and pray like the publican, "God, be merciful to me a sinner."

Here is another astonishing thing Paul says about faith. You will find it in his second letter to the Corinthians: "We walk by faith, not by sight." We are pilgrims plodding along a rough and dangerous road and we cannot depend on our eyes. That is a strange thing to say. What are our eyes for? Why should we not guide our course by appearance, by the things we see?

No, says Paul, we chart our course by another faculty. We do not depend on our physical senses. We walk by faith. We walk as Abraham walked. He went out, not knowing whither he went. Do you know where you are going in the next year? Do you know where you are going tomorrow? A heavy mist lies on the path; we see but one step at a time. We have to walk by faith or we cannot walk at all.

One hears it said that this is not an age of faith but an age of doubt, that it is difficult in a day like this to keep one's faith, that many are losing their faith. I wonder. One would suppose that when the world situation was black many would lose their faith. But curiously it is when the world is dark that the lamp of faith burns brightest. My reading of history leads me to believe that good times, easy times are bad times for faith; hard times, troublous times are good times for faith.

In Old Testament times it was when worst came to worst in the shattering experience of the Exile that the faith of the Hebrews rose to its highest. In New Testament times it was in the age of persecution when Christians were thrown to the beasts in the arena, or used as torches to light Nero's gardens, that their faith became heroic.

Some are disquieted by attacks on religion, especially those emanating from the intelligentsia. This brilliant professor tells his classes that the New Testament is a collection of legend and wish-thinking. This fluent writer publishes an article in which he declares that the doctrines of Christianity have been exploded. A woman, concerned about her college-age children, said to me, "Don't you know that all the advanced thinkers have given up Christianity? They do not believe in religion at all." Dear lady, if the advanced thinkers have given up Christianity, it is nothing new.

Many years ago, when I was a student at Columbia, I took Professor James Harvey Robinson's course, "The History of the Intellectual Class in Western Europe." I was reminded of it by a description of it in Irwin Edman's delightful book, *Philosopher's Holiday*. All through that famous course, which Professor Edman suggests might have been more aptly titled "The History of Human Stupidity," Professor Robinson sneered at religion in general and the Christian religion in particular, allowed his saturnine wit full play at its expense.

Edman tells of a woman student who complained to Professor Robinson, "You are taking away my faith." "But if I took away a headache," he replied, "you would not complain." Faith and a headache were all the same to him. But what chance has a brilliant scoffer against the religious sentiment in the hearts of plain people, the sentiment, for example, which clusters about Christmas, when men's hearts glow warm and tender as they think of the coming of the Christ into the world?

There is no living writer as excoriating as Voltaire. To Voltaire religion was a mass of superstition and religious people were fools. He prophesied that within a hundred years religion would be extinct and the churches crumbling to ruins. A hundred years afterward the room in which he wrote that prophecy was being used by a Bible society as a repository for newly printed Bibles, and more churches were being built than ever before.

What chance had a brilliant rationalist against the religious sentiment which clusters about Good Friday and Easter? Perhaps Voltaire sensed this. One day one of his disciples came to him in perplexity. He had founded a new religion from which all trace of the supernatural had been excluded. He was surprised that a religion so simple and reasonable had not swept the field. But people didn't seem to warm up to it. "If you were starting a new religion," he asked, "how would you go about it?" "I think," said Voltaire, "the best way would be to get yourself crucified and on the third day rise from the dead."

It is inevitable—I do not gloss it over—that in a day like ours the faith of many thoughtful people is sorely tried. Perhaps you have lost faith in God. Maybe he never was very real to you and such faith as you had in him was secondhand. You have lost faith in yourself. You are getting along pretty well, but sometimes you feel you are a fraud. You wonder what people would think of you if they should find you out. You have lost faith in your fellow men. Sometimes you talk cynically of the folly of trying to do right in a selfish world. You have lost faith in the good causes in which you once believed, such as world peace, world brotherhood, the world mission of Christianity. They seem futile in a world dominated by force and greed. You are often a puzzle to yourself; and when you lie awake at night and try to think it out, your thoughts go round in a circle. You say, "I wish I had a strong faith, which would give unity and direction to my life. But I cannot believe just because I want to believe. My faith must be supported by reason."

No one is more firmly committed to a reasonable faith than I am. It has long been one of my minor ambitions to make the old-time religion intellectually respectable, so to state it that it will appeal to reasonable people and stand up under reasonable criticism. But I submit that most of the beliefs we hold are not based primarily on reason. Certainly this is so of belief in God. When you take a course in the philosophy of religion you are given the so-called theistic proofs, the classic arguments for the existence of God: the ontological, the cosmological, the teleological and so on. They have their cogency, but it is not because of them that men have come to believe in God. They are afterthoughts, meant to justify to the reason what men had already come to believe on other grounds.

It is like falling in love. Does a young man say, "This girl is intelligent, capable, has a fine family background, we have many interests in common, I enjoy her company; therefore I will fall in love with her"? No, he falls in love first, then he gives himself reasons for doing what he has already done. So it is with faith in God: it is primarily a matter of instinct and emotion, an outreach of the personality. The main highway of belief in God runs back through Hebrew history, recorded in the Old Testament. In the Old Testament we find little trace of speculative reasoning concerning the existence of God. Faith in God came to this remarkable people through experience, through Israel's vicissitudes as a people from the Exodus to the Exile and, in the case of some, like Hosea and Jeremiah, through poignant personal experience. Reason is only one phase of experience.

Clement of Alexandria, one of the Greek church fathers who lived about the year 200, says that faith leads to knowledge, knowledge to love, and love unites the knower and the known. Said Augustine, one of the Latin church fathers who lived about the year 400, "I do not seek to know in order that I may believe, I seek to believe in order that I may know." Here are two of the greatest minds the church has had affirming that faith is the antecedent and prerequisite of knowledge, not the other way around.

The Roman Church teaches that the existence of God can be proved by logic. I do not think that is correct. God is too great to be fitted into our neat little formulae. I believe he has left it so that if we will we may believe and if we will we may disbelieve. If we could prove his existence, as we prove a theorem in geometry and write Q.E.D. at the end, if we could be sure of him in the same way we are sure of the things we touch and handle, there would be no room for this high faculty of the soul we call faith.

If we want to get the Biblical idea of faith, we cannot do better than to study the eleventh chapter of Hebrews. The writer begins by defining faith. But he realizes that faith cannot be defined; it can only be exhibited. It can be understood by looking at those who have it. So he passes in review a long procession of the heroes of faith. But he does not bid us keep our eyes on them. He bids us keep our eyes on Jesus, the supreme hero of faith.

Jesus believed in the goodness of God, though God did not allow him to escape the cross. He believed in the innate nobility of the human soul, though men hated him and crucified him. He believed that human life is immeasurably precious, though in his day as in ours it seemed cheap. He believed that with God all things are possible, that therefore what ought to be can be, what ought not be will finally be done away. Because of his faith in God he had faith in men. Because of his faith in men he had high and undiscourageable expectations of the future. In the last week of his life, knowing that men were about to kill him, he said, "I, when I am lifted up, will draw all men unto me." That is faith.

✠

Prayer

SINCE WE ARE surrounded by so great a cloud of witnesses, rally us to lay aside every weight and the sin that clings so closely and to run with perseverance the race that is set before us, looking to Jesus, the pioneer and perfecter of our faith, who for the joy that was set before him endured the cross, despising the shame. May his grace abide with us hour by hour and day by day. Amen.

VIII

Old Paths to Follow

Dr. Edgar DeWitt Jones says that the preacher today is in a curious position: industrialists and capitalists suspect him of being a parlor pink, while radicals of all hues openly regard him as the tool and mouthpiece of capitalism. The most flattering interpretation to put on this—and I hope the correct one—is that preachers have held to their course, preserved their independence of judgment, not allowed themselves to be dragooned by any group, with the result that they are neither as consistently liberal as their left-wing friends desire nor as ardent defenders of the *status quo* as their tory friends would approve.

In point of fact, I suspect that most people are neither rigid conservatives nor thoroughgoing liberals, but liberal and conservative by turn—liberal in regard to some matters, conservative in regard to others, liberal in some moods, conservative in others. For myself, I am a conservative by instinct and temperament; in some things I am a liberal by conviction. I have sometimes thought that I am unfitted to be a propagandist by a fatal propensity for seeing both sides of a question. To be an effective propagandist one should have a touch of fanaticism, the intensity that comes from seeing only one side. It is when one perceives that there are sound arguments and a sound emotional basis on both sides of most moot questions that "the native hue of resolution is sicklied o'er with the pale cast of thought."

It is more fun to be on one side or the other. In theology it must be exciting to be either an out-and-out modernist valiantly crusading for the newer positions, or a stalwart fundamentalist, standing like Horatius at the bridge to defend the faith once delivered to the saints against all comers. But if you happen to believe, as I do, that the truth lies between them, then there's nothing for you to do but keep to the middle of the road—an unexciting and unheroic position but with this possible advantage: it enables one to understand his friends on either hand and to interpret them to one another.

In Jeremiah 6:16 we read: "Stand by the road, and look, and ask for the old paths, where the good way is; and walk in it, and find rest for your souls."

Those sound like the words of an arch standpatter, which Jeremiah was anything but. He was a reformer, and the people hated him for it. On one occasion they flung him into prison. On another they threw him into a well. He loved his people but they did not love him. The fact that he proved right and they wrong did not increase their affection for him. He was always on the unpopular side.

He was not only a reformer; he was also an innovator. He was the author of a new idea in religion, a profoundly influential idea, the idea of the new covenant, written not on tablets of stone but on the heart; the idea that all true reform proceeds not from outside in but from inside out, that the only law which can save men is a law written not in statute books but in the heart, a living relation between a man and God.

This idea of the new covenant was congenial to Jesus. He adopted it. He was thinking of Jeremiah when on the last night of his life he said, "This cup is the new covenant in my blood." Jeremiah was a reformer and an innovator, but Jeremiah saw that the people of his day were getting away from things which their fathers had tried and found good, were flouting the dear-bought experience of many generations; and so he bade them to seek old paths to follow.

Without pausing to specify what the people of his day were repudiating, I jump at once from Jerusalem of the sixth century B.C. to America of the twentieth century A.D. and express the conviction that we Americans are going back on certain ideas in which we've always believed, ideas which have been tried and proved good.

One is the idea that *work is a blessing*. Man's earliest reaction to the stern necessity of "bread labor," as Tolstoi called it, was to regard it as a curse and punishment, the penalty for sin. This is the idea reflected in the story of man's expulsion from the Garden of Eden: "In the sweat of your face you shall eat bread till you return to the ground." If man had not sinned, if he had not offended God, he would not have had to work.

This idea lingered long. In England even two hundred years ago the gentleman was the man who did not have to work. Like the nobility of old China, he allowed his fingernails to grow long to prove to the world that his hands were not sullied by toil.

Here in America a different philosophy of work has evolved—the idea that work is not a curse nor yet an expedient, something we do in order to purchase a certain amount of leisure, but a blessing. By work a man's faculties are developed: manual skill by working with the hands, mental keenness and grasp by working with the brain. By work a man earns his living and takes his place among effective and useful human beings. By work he expresses the serious and responsible purpose of his life. By work the crude material of his nature is wrought into character. Work transforms the material worked on. It transforms the worker also. What a man makes out of his work is important. What his work makes out of him is more important.

Picture to yourself the difference between this planet as it is today and as it was ten thousand years ago. What has made the difference? Work. Labor plus imagination equals civilization. And the difference between the world then and now corresponds to the difference between man then and now. The history of art provides a ready illustration. The first attempt at art was probably the scratching with some rude instrument, perhaps a sharp stone, on the tusk of an elephant or the bone of some large animal; or it was the drawing of rude figures on the wall of a cave. Man's aesthetic sense grew as he tried to express the beauty he saw, until it became dissatisfied and demanded something finer. So step by step art developed, till from these crude beginnings we have Phidias, Michelangelo, Rodin and all the beauty which they and their fellow craftsmen have brought into the world. Men have transformed the world by their labor and at the same time have transformed themselves.

If you want to improve yourself, improve your work. Most of us would be dwarfs except for what our work has made of us. Little tasks breed little men. Great tasks breed great men, for they call forth all our powers. Each day's work is a challenge to be met, a victory to be won. Says Dean Inge:

"There are few purer sources of happiness than the consciousness of having made or produced something good of its kind. The happy people are those who are producing something; the bored people are those who are consuming much and producing nothing. God punishes the useless by giving them pleasure without joy, and very dull they find it."

A man's work is his life preserver in a bigger sense than that it preserves him from starvation and keeps him out of mischief. It is work that makes life worth living. This nation can have no aristocracy except an aristocracy of workmanship, of those who do hard and necessary things and do them well.

Such is the American philosophy of work, a philosophy which has grown up here from the pioneer days when men subdued the wilderness and made it to blossom like the rose. I do not say we have always lived up to it, but this is what we have believed.

Today we are cultivating another philosophy. It is implied in such phrases as "the more abundant life," "the new leisure," "the shorter workday," "the thirty-hour week." Underlying all these phrases is the assumption that work is an evil to be reduced to its minimum and the absence of work a good to be enlarged to its maximum.

All the effective business executives I know are hard-working. So are all the best professional men I know. Many of our top government officials are prodigious workers. All the learned men I know burn the midnight oil; with all our modern short cuts and mechanical devices, there is still no royal road to learning. The men we admire, the men who get the world on, the men who win true success in any field are workers.

Nonetheless there has grown up the philosophy of a new Utopia in which hard work is to be avoided: don't do as much as you can, do as little as you can. Men in the building crafts are not the only ones who deliberately restrict their output. The doctrine has spread far. It is not only false, it is pernicious, especially to young men. A few of them realize it.

None of the technological nor economic changes of the past few years alters the fact that there is work to be done in the world and the only limit to this work is men's willingness and capacity to do it. Mankind lives on what it produces. The more it produces, the more it can consume. There is no other source of goods for consumption. If men decided tomorrow to produce half as much, our standard of living would drop, for we should have half as much to consume. Wealth is the result of labor applied to material—to the soil, to a coal mine, to a bar of steel or a bolt of cloth. No wealth is produced by the fluctuations of the stock market or by betting on a horse race. Wealth is produced by labor applied to material.

In science, in research, in government there is no limit to the work to be done. If a young man acquires competence, he will find more work for his hands to do than there are hours in the day to do it. More than that, the capacity to create, the opportunity to make your business, your profession, your city a little better because you have worked in it satisfies one of the basic instincts of human nature. We don't want America to become a nation of coupon clippers at one end of the scale and reliefers at the other, parasites both. When that day arrives, we can write above the portal of America, "Ichabod"—the glory is departed. Let us not go back on the American philosophy of work.

Just as we are getting away from the idea that industry is a virtue, so we are getting away from the idea that *thrift is a virtue*. What is thrift? Thrift is not merely enthusiasm for a savings account. Thrift is the conservation of the material blessings of life by the proper care of them.

I have not much of the lust for ownership. I had rather be able to walk around a beautiful city park than to have an estate of my own. I had rather have access to the Art Museum than to have an art gallery of my own. I am glad that some of my friends have big houses, big gardens, old masters, first editions, antiques, but I do not covet them. Even if I had the means to acquire them, I should not want them, for I do not want to spend most of my working hours managing property. I do not envy people the possession of things so precious they must be kept in a safe-deposit box, to which at intervals they make furtive expeditions to see if they're still there. One woman I knew had a pearl necklace so costly she never dared wear it; she kept it tucked away in a hiding place, while she wore a replica of imitation pearls. I do not collect anything—not even books. When I am through with a book I either give it away or lend it—which usually comes to the same thing. I say this to indicate that property is not my god.

I go on to say that there is a screw loose in the man who does not have a decent regard for property. There is something wrong with the man who is careless with money, for money always represents labor, his own or someone else's. Money is minted lifeblood; that is why the arbitrary devaluation of money is a cruel and unjust thing.

There is something wrong with the man who is careless with property, for someone has worked to produce or acquire it, has exchanged for it so many hours or days of his life.

There is something wrong with the man who does not have a feeling of respect for an object which would never have been if the intelligence and skill of some man or of many men had not gone into its making.

There is something wrong with the farmer who leaves his tools unsheltered in all kinds of weather, with the man who abuses the motorcar in which he has invested part of his savings. There is something wrong with the person who defaces or mutilates a book, with boys and girls who leave their bicycles out in the rain or who at Halloween wantonly destroy the property of others. When we read that Napoleon stabled his horse in the Chapel of Santa Maria della Grazia in Milan we know that with all his brilliance there was a quirk in his make-up: he wasn't all there.

Vandalism may be described as the taste for messing up things that belong to others, things which the vandal has not the wit to appreciate. The cure for it is to train him in the care of things of which he does know the value. Children should be taught respect for property by being given property of their own and trained to take care of it. As soon as possible they should be taught the wise use of money—how to earn, how to save, how to spend, how to give. They should be helped to realize that the best things we have we have because we have learned to appreciate them.

I grow a little weary of the people who are always talking about "human rights" as distinguished from "property rights," as though the two were set over against each other. What are "property rights" except human rights in property? There is something mystical, almost sacramental, about the possession of property.

My eye ranges over the rows of books on the shelves before

me. Of course to me they are something more than so much ink and paper. They represent the winnowed wisdom and truth of the ages, the priceless heritage of the race. Do I own my books? Only in the sense that they are mine to use. I hold them for a while, then I pass on and the books remain. My greatest content in thinking of them is that they are superior to my ownership. They, not I, are masters of destiny so far as this earth is concerned.

Many years ago the lady who shares my fortunes and I bought a little plot on a hillside overlooking a lake. With mattock and ax we cleared it of underbrush and grubbed out the stumps. We set out trees, evergreens, flowering shrubs. Summer after summer we have had the joy of cultivating them and watching them grow. Do we own that plot of ground? Only in that it is ours to use. Presently we shall pass on and others will use it, enjoy the sweet scent of the lilacs we planted, regale themselves with looking out across the lake to the hills beyond. My greatest satisfaction in thinking of that plot is that it is superior to my ownership. When I pass on, it will remain for others to enjoy.

The burial office in the Book of Common Prayer contains these words: "We brought nothing into the world, and we cannot carry anything out." That verse is not often read at funerals nowadays, for to our squeamish modern taste it sounds grim. I do not find it so. To me it is not grim but comforting to reflect that though I brought nothing into the world, so much has been given me to use and to enjoy that when I pass on, the things I have made and those which other men have made for me will continue to enrich other lives.

Our discussion of thrift has taken us far afield, but all that has been said follows from the thought of thrift as the conservation of material blessings. I pass over more obvious aspects of the subject: the sin of waste, extravagance, ostentation in a world where many want; the folly of living beyond one's means; the thriftlessness of mortgaging one's future earnings by installment buying, which is one of the major evils of present-day America.

The patron saint of thrift is Benjamin Franklin. Once when a savings bank was using his picture and some of the pithy sayings from *Poor Richard's Almanack* in its advertising, someone remarked that Franklin was "the great American tightwad." Anyone who has read his life knows that, far from being parsimonious, Franklin was one of the most generous of men, a princely giver to institutions and good causes. Had he been a wastrel and a spendthrift, he could not have been a philanthropist. It was because he had learned how to earn and how to save that he was able to give. Let us not go back on the virtue of thrift.

Another idea in which America has long believed but which is called in question today is the idea of *mass education*. One of the best things we have done here in America is to develop universal free education at public expense, so that to any boy or girl who has the requisite health and ambition the avenues of education are open from kindergarten to university. We have assumed that the salvation of a democracy is an informed and educated electorate. The faith which underlies democracy is that if you open the avenues of education freely to all, you will get some surprising results from unexpected quarters. And that faith has been vindicated.

One of my right-hand men in a church I formerly served was an Armenian. He had come to this country as a boy, educated himself by working days and going to night school, been admitted to the bar and made assistant prosecutor of one of the most populous counties in America. He was a most capable and conscientious public official, fearless in the performance of his duty but with a sense of personal responsibility for the men whom he helped put in prison and those out on parole. All of you could give similar instances, and we used to like to say a little boastfully, "That could happen only in America."

Today some sophisticates disparage mass education, compare it to its disadvantage with the old aristocratic idea of education, quote Dr. Mayo to the effect that many are being "educated beyond their intelligence," assert that the graduates of our great state universities lack intellectual distinction and are as standardized as the automobiles now coming off the assembly lines. Poppycock! Isn't mass education just what we want? What hope is there for America if the masses are not educated? We don't want "the mass mind," to be sure, but I fail to see how the mass mind is produced by sending people to school and college and exposing them to ideas and the history of ideas.

You get the mass mind when you fail to expose men to ideas and their history and so leave them the prey of every demagogue who comes along, because they have no background against which to criticize and appraise. A few may be "educated beyond their intelligence," but many are not yet educated up to their intelligence. There lies our unfinished task: to see to it that every American boy and girl has as much education as he is capable of accepting, to keep our public-school system right up to par. Let us not go back on our American idea of mass education.

One more idea is part of our American tradition: *freedom*

of worship. Of course the struggle for freedom of worship is older than America. You know something of John Huss, who was burned in Constance, Bohemia, in 1415; of Hugh Latimer and Nicholas Ridley, who were burned in Oxford in 1555; of the Waldenses, the followers of Peter Waldo, who were hunted and hounded throughout Italy until finally they found a refuge in the Alpine valleys southwest of Turin; of the Huguenots and their great leader, Admiral Coligny, of the long and cruel persecution they endured, culminating in the massacre of St. Bartholomew's Day in 1572.

You know more about the Puritan movement in England, because it is intimately related to our own history. It was a protest against the corruption of the Church of England. It assumed such proportions that in 1604 King James I called a conference at Hampton Court between the bishops and the Puritans, at which he heard so many distasteful things that he broke up the conference in wrath, saying of the nonconformists, "I will make them conform or I will harry them out of the land."

You know something about the Separatists, who were left-wing Puritans, for whereas the Puritans hoped to reform the Church of England from within, the Separatists felt that the abuses were too many and too great and their only recourse was to leave it.

The *Mayflower* Pilgrims were Separatists. They believed it was their right as believers in Jesus Christ to worship God according to their own conscience. This idea ran counter to the general belief of the time, for Englishmen on the whole believed in uniformity and made life miserable for any who did not fall in line. It was to secure freedom of worship that the Pilgrims sought these shores. I know the debunking historians will tell you they came in the hope of improving their economic status. Human motives are mixed and that desire may have been present. But no fair-minded person can study the facts without seeing that it was the desire to find freedom of worship which impelled the Pilgrims to go first to Holland and then to America.

The Plymouth Colony, the Massachusetts Bay Colony, the Hartford and New Haven colonies were founded by men who sought freedom of worship. Rhode Island was founded by Baptists under Roger Williams, seeking freedom of worship. Pennsylvania was settled by Quakers under William Penn who sought freedom of worship for themselves and granted religious toleration to those who dissented from them. Maryland was founded by Catholics under Lord Baltimore: they too sought freedom of worship for themselves and granted religious toleration to those who dissented from them. The Carolinas were settled by the Covenanters, Scotch-Irish Presbyterians, who sought freedom of worship.

The idea of freedom of worship was deeply ingrained in our American tradition before our life as a nation began. When the Constitution was written it guaranteed freedom of worship to all our citizens.

In our day multitudes have construed freedom of worship to mean freedom not to worship. Thousands of professing Christians, by their desultory church attendance and their casual attitude when they come, betray how lightly they esteem the privilege which is theirs. It is a different attitude from theirs whose religious convictions were so strong that they endured persecution, confiscation of property, imprisonment, exile, death rather than go back on them and who by their insistence won our religious liberty for us. It means something to you that you can gather in your church on Sunday to worship God according to your own conscience and that your neighbors of other faiths can do the same. Don't abuse a privilege that has heroism and sacrifice written all over it. Cherish it. Revere it. Teach your children to revere it. Don't go back on the American idea of freedom of worship.

The journey of life is a strange adventure, and our lives have not been set in an easy time. We feel with the Israelites that we "have not passed this way before." Old landmarks have been uprooted. Old moral codes have lost their grip. Two world wars and the atom bomb have given civilization a jolt from which it is still reeling. Clouds and darkness are round about us. We know not what the morrow holds for us, our nation or our world.

But despite the changes, it is not really a new world. Permanent acquisitions have come to man which neither we nor our children will go back on: philosophy, above all the Christian revelation; art as it flowered in the age of Phidias and the Italian Renaissance; literature as it became articulate in such world voices as Homer and Virgil, Dante and Shakespeare; science with all it has taught us about this world which is our home. These are a permanent part of the race's inheritance.

Revolutions, after all, are shallow things, and civilization emerges from them holding intact the things which have been tried and found good. We have considered four: the blessedness of work, the virtue of thrift, education for all as a pillar of democratic government, freedom in the worship of God. "Ask for the old paths, where the good way is; and walk in it, and find rest for your souls."

Prayer

We were born to a great tradition and we would not weaken it by our indolence or folly. Rally us to prove worthy of it and to pass all the best of it to our children. So may grace, mercy and peace from God our Father and the Lord Jesus Christ be and abide with us evermore. Amen.

IX

The Lord's Work

THE minor prophets are among the least known books of the Bible. And no wonder. They are not easy to understand. Plain folk who want to know what the message of the Bible is are baffled by them; find themselves in a strange world where they cannot proceed without an interpreter.

Consider, for example, the third and last chapter of the little book with the uneuphonious name of Habakkuk. "God came from Teman." What does that mean? Why did the curtains of the land of Midian tremble? Some give it up as beyond them. Others consult the commentaries and learn what the scholars say. Others skip what is obscure, concentrating on what is clear—and fortunately there are verses as simple as they are sublime.

Such passages are difficult for the preacher, too. He knows they yield their meaning only to those who dig into them, that there is much to explain which is well worth explaining. But many are not interested in ancient literature, may grow impatient, complain that he is remote from practical concerns. Therefore I confine myself to a thumbnail introduction.

Probably this splendid ode, this stirring poetical description of God's march from Sinai to help his people, was not written by the prophet Habakkuk but by a later poet who lived in equally critical days. It voices the same unfaltering trust in God despite dismaying circumstance which was Habakkuk's great conviction. Writing material was costly and scarce; there was some space left on the scroll, so the copyist added this eschatological psalm.

Every crisis is a day of judgment. The word *crisis* comes from the Greek verb which means "to judge." When dangers thicken, when the traditions and systems which in calm weather seem permanent break into fragments, the thoughts of many hearts are revealed. The scoffer scoffs. The cynic gives vent to his cynicism. The man of faith turns to God. The more the earth trembles, the more he finds in God his refuge and his strong tower. This poet was a deeply religious man. There were scoffers and cynics around him. Perhaps he had moods of skepticism and despair, but he rises above them and calls upon God to reveal himself amid the turmoil:

> O Lord, revive thy work in the midst of the years,
> In the midst of the years make it known.

Here is a prayer we may well make our own. Ours is a critical time. Men like to say they live in an age of transition—a platitudinous remark which sounds profound. Every age is an age of transition. Sir Gilbert Murray tells of a cuneiform inscription on a tablet uncovered in the lowest stratum of the ruins of Babylon, said to be the oldest piece of writing extant. It begins: "Alas, times are not what they were."

But though all times are times of transition, the pace varies from slow to fast. Today it is fast and the changes are sweeping. More progress in applied science was made in the past century than in all the centuries preceding. From the dawn of history to the time of Napoleon inclusive, man's swiftest mode of travel was the horse. Then came the locomotive, the motorcar, the airplane. Now we read of the supersonic plane—a plane traveling faster than sound.

Till just over a century ago (1844), man's swiftest mode of communication was by mail or courier. It took mail months to reach the remote parts of the world. Then came telegraph communication by dots and dashes through a charged wire; then the telephone, the human voice transmitted through a charged wire; then the radio, enabling men to hear each other's voices half a world away by a more sensitive medium of transmission than a charged wire—the ether wave.

Today we are still oppressed by war weariness, in the trough of reaction from a long, nerve-racking ordeal; but in quiet laboratories the country over patient scientists are working out the implications and applications of nuclear fission, which may turn out to be not the most sinister but the most beneficent of discoveries. And those best in a position to know say we are on the threshold of an age whose possibilities for advance are beyond the imagination.

The speed of transition may be illustrated by an excerpt from the State of the Union message which President Coolidge delivered to the Seventieth Congress in December 1928:

No Congress ever assembled has met with a more pleasing prospect than that which appears at the present time. In the domestic field there is tranquillity and contentment, harmonious relations between management and wage earner, freedom from industrial strife, and the highest prosperity. In the foreign field there is peace, the good will which comes from mutual understanding, and the knowledge that the problems which a short time ago appeared so ominous are yielding to the touch of manifest friendship. The great wealth created by our enterprise and industry and saved by our economy has had the widest distribution among our own people and has gone out in a steady stream to serve the charity and business of the world. The requirements of existence have passed beyond the standard of necessity into the region of luxury. Enlarging production is consumed by an increasing demand at home and an expanding commerce abroad. The country can regard the present with satisfaction and the future with optimism.

Since Mr. Coolidge painted this rosy picture the United States and the world have gone through their worst depression and their most costly and destructive war. One need only to mention such trouble spots as Korea, China, Indo-China, Formosa, India, Pakistan, Iran, Palestine, Egypt, the continent of Africa seething with unrest from the Mediterranean to the Cape, to indicate why it is harder to "regard the present with satisfaction and the future with optimism" than when Mr. Coolidge used those confident words at the fag end of what Allan Nevins calls "the heroic age of American enterprise," with the collapse of the stock market only months away.

After the First World War there was much talk of "reverting to a prewar status"—"back to normalcy," in President Harding's phrase. One doesn't hear that today. No intelligent person expects a return to the *status quo*. My guess is that the Arnold Toynbees of the future will treat the Great Depression, the Second World War and the struggle of subject peoples for independence as phases of a world-wide social, economic and political revolution.

Everywhere the swift, unpredictable changes have created a sense of instability. Men do not know what to believe when what they thought was solid rock turns out to be shifting sand. The general uncertainty has invaded religion. A careful historian declares that the difference between the most enlightened Christian thought today and that of fifty years ago is more radical than that which separated Luther from the Pope.

Yet in the midst of the confusion, the disappointment that nineteen hundred years after Christ we are no farther along, certain convictions are emerging. One is that only in religion shall we find firm footing in a changing world. Another is that it must be a religion free from superstition, hypocrisy and worldliness, a religion rooted in the eternal mysteries but enunciating definite principles and calling on men and nations to walk in their light. With such convictions, what more fitting than that there be constantly on our lips this prayer:

> O Lord, revive thy work in the midst of the years,
> In the midst of the years make it known.

It is not enough to pray for revelation and revival. We must ask how far we can answer our own prayer. Immediately we come to this: we must seek revival first in our own souls.

We who love liberty are appalled by the way in which a

totalitarian country attempts to control the lives of its citizens: not only what they may do, but what they may read, what they may think, to what radio programs they may listen, what kind of music their composers may and may not compose, what theory of genetics their biologists may and may not hold. Yet we cannot help being impressed by the fact that communism, although antireligious and atheistic, has behind it the driving force of a religious passion, so that its devotees stop at nothing to attain their ends.

If we sang our hymns of faith with the fervor with which communists sing the "Internationale," the world would begin to suspect we believed what we were singing.

The only effective way we can meet this challenge is by proclaiming and demonstrating a better society: the true community of the family of God, the free growth of personality within a community of free men. We Christians, despite our broken hopes, believe that Christ can so transform human society as to make possible a world community, a family of interdependent nations in an ordered world. But it comes back to the individual. Says a British statesman: "To believe in a change in human nature may be an act of faith; to believe in a change in human society without a change in human nature is an act of lunacy." No permanent reformation is ever imposed from without; all true reformation proceeds from within. The soul of reformation is the reformation of the soul.

When men outside the church reproach it for its lack of influence, we could give them an argument but perhaps we do better to keep still. If every professing Christian took his religion as seriously as I take mine but no more, how much influence would religion have in the world? Would it be strong enough to move mountains? Perhaps we need look no farther for an explanation of the church's weakness.

In a day when not yellow journalists but responsible scientists are warning us of the consequence of an atomic war against which there is no defense and in which there is no place to hide, when General MacArthur at the Japanese surrender said that our chief problems are not military but theological, some of us are playing with our religion, a religion which has a cross at its core, a cross on which a man once hung until he died because he wasn't playing.

A thoughtful man once asked me what proportion of the community was unrelated to any church. I answered that I couldn't hazard a guess but that all through my ministry people I did not know had phoned to arrange for a wedding or a funeral and to my question, "Have you any other church connection?" answered, "No."

Then he asked why in a high-grade community, one of the finest residential areas in America, there should be a considerable number unrelated to the church. There are many reasons, some uncomplimentary to those who hold aloof not only from the church but from everything which keeps a community from going to rot. But perhaps one reason they have not been attracted to the church is because they see it makes so little difference in the lives of those who do belong or because no one has taken the trouble to invite them.

We respect the faith of our fathers. We regard the church as an essential institution. We contribute to its support. But too often our attitude is that of patrons of it rather than partners in it; our religion is a polite acquiescence rather than a passion and a power. We regret the wrong we have done, the sorrow we have caused others, but we have never really repented and determined to clean up our lives. We have joined with others in acts of devotion but we have seldom prayed with all our heart.

We have known religion as a comforting or restraining influence; we have never experienced what the men of the Bible mean when they say that "our God is a consuming fire." It has touched the fringe of our conduct; it has not penetrated the depths of our souls, impelling us to say with Augustine, "I tremble and I burn: I tremble, knowing I am unlike him; I burn, knowing I am like him." Our religion has been too impersonal. This is the source of our spiritual poverty. And I can think of no more fitting prayer as we set out on another stage of our journey than this: "O Lord, revive thy work in the midst of the years, beginning with me."

Only God can renew his work. And he who has brought us up out of savagery, out of cruel rites and dark superstitions, he who sent his son into the world for us and our salvation, will not desert us now. But we can prepare the way by giving all we have and are to the strengthening of our Christian fellowship. We want more friendship, more sharing of experience, more bearing of one another's burdens. Nothing impressed the ancient world more than the brotherliness of the early Christians. One of their keenest opponents, Celsus, spoke of them with bitterness and scorn, yet confessed, "They recognize one another by secret marks and signs, loving each other almost before they are acquainted." This was what drew men to the church in its early, heroic days, when it swept across the Roman Empire and nothing could hold it back. This is what will draw men to it today. It is a cold world and men are drawn to a fire.

In the midst of the world's distress, when men's hearts faint and fail, let us pray without ceasing for a new outpouring of God's spirit. Let us help to answer our prayer by taking our religion seriously, accepting God's grace, brothering Christ's people, giving gladly what we have to give, receiving gladly what is given us, building the inner shrine, setting the cross up in the heart. And even in a shadowed world and a terrific time we shall have a foretaste of his eternal kingdom of love and peace and joy.

Prayer

Eternal Spirit of the living God, who knowest the way into our inmost souls, where thou canst bring peace to those who are troubled, light to those who are confused, courage to those who are afraid, once again we gather in this house of prayer to link our lives with thine. It is not mere habit which brings us here but a hunger unappeased, a thirst unslaked apart from thee. We thank thee that thou art always accessible, most near when we most deeply feel our need of thee.

Help us in these trying days to bear our own burden manfully but not to try to carry thine; to remember that when we have done our best we may confidently leave the rest with thee; that the major responsibility for this beautiful but shadowed world rests with thee; that long before we came into it thou were at work on thine age-long purposes, using men and women like ourselves to further them; that long after our brief moment of life is done thou wilt be working still, patiently shaping the world nearer to thy heart's desire; that all thou dost ask of us is to put our lives on the highest level we can reach and resolutely keep them there, meeting life's varied problems with all the intelligence and courage we possess.

Teach us to be practical idealists with our eyes on the stars and our feet on the ground, never losing sight of the ideal but willing to work toward it with whatever instruments are at hand, however broken or imperfect they may be. Teach us to think of life as a race to be won, a series of crises to be met—met bravely, hopefully, with no trace of self-pity or self-distrust. Teach us to work happily under pressure, to eliminate needless worries and strains. Give us an inner composure which is beyond the reach of circumstance.

Guard us in our low moods, our hours of temptation and despair. Help us then to set a seal upon our lips, lest by any cynical or ill-considered words we blight another's faith or poison the air another must breathe. In reckless hours, in moods of depletion, of the spirit's ebb tide, recall us to ourselves by the thought of those who love and trust us and expect great things of us.

We crave a more abundant life than the partial life we now know. Thou seest how disparate are our dreams and our powers—our dreams, how glorious! our powers, how puny and frail! May thy liberating spirit move through the sluggish currents of our being. Quicken our perceptions. Clarify our thinking. Cleanse our imagination. Stiffen our will. Help us to live on a plane where the petty discords and jealousies of our self-regard can find no place. Give us a closer walk with thee.

Once again and altogether we commit ourselves to the ancient loyalties, the Christian obedience and the Christian service. Father, into thy hands we commit our spirits this day and evermore, serene and sure in the faith that thou meanest nought but good to thy children, that thou wilt keep him in perfect peace whose mind is stayed on thee, that in this world and the world to which we go the eternal God is our refuge and underneath are the everlasting arms. Amen.

X

Finding Strength in Weakness

One evening I sat on a platform beside a prominent man who was known as an independent thinker, a bold and forthright speaker. He was there to speak on an important issue. When he rose to speak he was in complete command of himself; but before he was called upon and after he had finished, his hands trembled violently. It was a symptom of extreme nervousness. I wondered if the audience realized how much that speech, which impressed us by its sincerity and directness, cost him.

Sir Henry Irving said he seldom went on the stage without feeling nervous and when he did the performance fell flat. Many whom we account heroes have been keenly sensitive to danger, brave not because they felt no fear but because they learned first to control and then to conquer it. One of Napoleon's marshals, looking down at his trembling knees before a charge, exclaimed, "Shake, will you? You'd shake more if you knew where I am going to take you!" John Knox confessed he often felt timid as a mouse. But John Knox stood before a wicked queen and told her plain truths that no one else in her kingdom dared to tell her.

It is one thing to be a bully by nature and another to refuse to be bullied by one's nature. Someone has said that every heart is an arena where a hero and a coward wage continual conflict for mastery. On its outcome hinge our self-respect, our usefulness, our happiness. It is no sham battle. None of us is so courageous he has not felt the emotion of fear, none so craven he does not long to meet danger and disaster like a man.

Measured by ability and influence, Paul is one of the foremost figures of history. It was he who carried the Christian religion from Asia, the continent where it arose, to Europe, the continent from which our ancestors came. He wrote the most valuable letters ever written. They are the earliest Christian writings that have come down to us, the only writings we have from the first Christian generation.

Paul had suffered martyrdom before Mark, our earliest gospel, was written. He was not only the earliest of the New Testament writers; he was the most prolific. Thirteen of its twenty-seven books are attributed to him. Gilbert Murray of Oxford, foremost Hellenist of our time, says that Paul is certainly one of the towering figures of Greek literature—no mean distinction for one who was not a Greek but a Jew and only incidentally a writer.

He did more than anyone else to formulate Christian thought. It has been said truly that the two supreme facts of Christian history are the experience of God in the soul of Jesus and the experience of Jesus in the soul of Paul. He is the greatest follower and truest interpreter Jesus has ever had. He was a daring adventurer, a lionhearted pioneer.

He could take hard knocks and come back for more. Imprisonment, scourging, shipwreck, stoning, exposure, hunger were all in the day's work for him. Yet, writing to the Corinthians, this intrepid man says, "I was with you in weakness and in much fear and trembling."

There can be no doubt of his sincerity. He was too much of a man to be insincere. Nor was he given to undue self-disparagement. Near the end, as he looked back on his life, he did not hesitate to say what—please God—you and I may be able to say when our course is run, "I have fought the good fight . . . I have kept the faith." Yet he confesses he was no stranger to weakness and fear.

Most of those who have helped the world on would say the same. Here and there a man may say, "I am the master of my fate, I am the captain of my soul." Those words are from a famous lyric which has been set to stirring music. The aim of a lyric, as students of literature know, is to express a single mood, a wave of feeling. Such a mood does not last. A slight displacement of the retina of the eye, a tiny speck on a lung, a sudden pain in the side, a feeling of dizziness—and there is an end to such boasting.

Wise men own their weakness, but the wisest have found a source of strength. "I was with you in weakness and in much fear and trembling," but "by the grace of God I am what I am. . . . I can do all things through him who strengthens me."

Surely this brings us comfort. When we are depressed by a sense of unworthiness and failure, it rallies us to know that the experience is not confined to us. It is shared by all who have striven for an ideal. The attainment of strength is nearly always the result of conquering weakness. No one was ever born a saint.

Someone asked, "Why were the saints saints?" and answered, "Because they were cheerful when it was hard to be cheerful, patient when it was hard to be patient; because they pushed on when they wanted to stay still, kept quiet when they wanted to talk, were agreeable when they felt like being disagreeable."

Those we most admire for the strength and consistency of their character have won it through weakness and fear. The Christian religion is for those who know they are weak, not those who think they are supermen. But some of us feel our weakness so keenly we allow it to paralyze us instead of impelling us to overcome it.

It was finely said of the scientists of the nineteenth century that they made their obstacles their steppingstones. So we can make our very weakness a steppingstone in the upward and difficult way.

Joseph Szigeti, famed violinist, was a child prodigy who was taught by his ambitious father to play dazzling show-off pieces like Paganini's "Witches' Dance" and Tartini's "Devil's Trill." As he grew older he became a touring virtuoso, exploiting his talent, playing to make money. In his early twenties he developed tuberculosis and had to spend three years taking a rest cure in the Swiss Alps.

He came under the care of a lung specialist who was passionately fond of music. To pay for his treatment he had only to play duets with his doctor. With a fresh batch of scores arriving every other week from a circulating library in Zurich, the two explored the whole field with emphasis on Beethoven, Mozart and Bach. During these years of enforced leisure Szigeti made a clean break with his prodigy past. When he came down from his mountain retreat his aim was not to make money but to make music. Before, his music had been a livelihood. From now on it was a fulfillment. He is known and honored for his dedication to the highest ideal of his art.

A seeming setback proved a steppingstone. Out of weakness came strength.

Three things a recognition of our weakness does for us. First, it keeps us humble, keeps us from saying like little Jack Horner, "What a great boy am I!" or "Mine own right arm hath gotten me the victory."

Second, it makes us sympathetic with the weakness of others. Brilliant students rarely make good teachers. They don't know the difficulties. Strong and clear in their own conceptions, they have scant patience with those who must grope their way. The plodding mind which must go over a thing again and again is a nuisance and a bore to those who get things the first time. But we can't despise those who have the same difficulties we have or once had. If we recognize our own faults, we can't be too hard on the faults of others. Feeling the weight of our own burdens, we want to help others to carry theirs.

And third, a sense of weakness leads us or drives us to God. When the sun is shining, when we are prosperous and successful, feel we are strong enough to do what we want to do and to push hindrances aside, we are likely to forget him. Why should we remember him when we are quite sufficient unto ourselves? But when dark and cruel days come, when we know failure and defeat, then we reach out a hand to clasp his—and our weakness is transmuted into strength.

We too may work out our own salvation with fear and trembling. The invalid may live longer than the athlete. Tennyson's health was so poor when a young man that his life was despaired of. By working out a regimen that agreed with him he lived to be eighty-three. He wrote his best-known, best-loved poem, "Crossing the Bar," when he was eighty. By ordering his life, an invalid may live out his years in better than average health.

The weakest organ in the body by care and exercise may become the strongest. Our vices may be transformed into virtues. Men who have been quick-tempered and irascible have become gentle and forbearing. First they learned to control their temper, then to triumph over it.

One of the most genial men I know confided to me that he was naturally morose and pessimistic. He said he had always assumed his besetting sin was one of the faults of body or mind which Paul calls "the works of the flesh." Against these he had struggled. But in a moment of insight it flashed upon him that his besetting sin was a habitual despondency which prevented his seeing how God had blessed and used him, and which kept him in a state of depression about his work, himself and the world. He saw how this dejected and dispirited attitude had saddened those who loved him and hindered his influence by creating an atmosphere of gloom. Whereupon he asked God's forgiveness and set out again as a prisoner of hope. He strove so earnestly to overcome his inclination to look on the dark side of things that he became one of the sunniest men I know. His weakness was transmuted into strength.

When I heard him make this confession, I had the uncomfortable feeling that he was getting close to where I live, that in exposing his own weakness he had exposed mine. Some of you may feel the same way, may come to see—as he came to see—that Christ means us to win the world by the light on our faces and the joy in our hearts, echoing his mighty assurance, "In the world you have tribulation; but be of good cheer, I have overcome the world." If you believe that, there was never a better time for the followers of Jesus to practice it than now.

It is in struggling against our infirmities that we develop our powers. Said Charles Darwin, "If I had not been so great an invalid, I should not have accomplished nearly so much work." Some time ago I read an article by Dr. Alfred Adler, the thesis of which was that the sense of inadequacy we call an inferiority complex is not a liability but an asset.

A wellborn, well-favored, normal youth, endowed with charm, good looks, native intelligence, to whom popularity, lessons, athletic prowess and social grace come easily, is usually lacking in intensity, rarely pushes himself. Why should he? The result is: he tends to become a dilettante, to trade on his amiable disposition, "get by on his personality." Whereas the youth who is conscious that he lacks good looks, charm, *savoir-faire,* to whom popularity does not come readily, endeavors to compensate for his deficiencies by achieving excellence in some realm which will give him a sense of worth. Dr. Adler cited instances of men eminent in many fields who were afflicted with a sense of inferiority but to whom it acted not as a brake but a spur, as they sought to transcend the limitations of their endowment by the wholeheartedness of their effort.

It is as we fight against our handicaps that we develop our powers. The strength of the lion, the agility of the leopard, the endurance of the camel, the swiftness of the hare have been built up by an unending struggle against difficulties and disadvantages in their environment and in themselves. The saintliness of the saints has been produced in the same way. Pain has issued in patience and fortitude, weakness has flowered into sympathy and skill.

We face the future in no bumptious spirit but in a chastened mood, knowing not what the morrow will bring to us and to our troubled world, whether peace or war or continuous uncertainty; knowing only that there are problems before us which we have not solved and that their solution will call for all the intelligence and self-control we can muster. It is when we are in this mood—most conscious of our weakness and inadequacy—that God can do the most in us, through us, for us.

Paul tells the Corinthians how he had come among them in weakness, in much fear and trembling. Yet it was in the notoriously wicked city of Corinth which he entered with misgiving and trepidation—as well he might—that he wrought his greatest moral miracles in Jesus' name. He catalogues the most vicious and depraved elements in the city, people guilty of unspeakable abominations and unnatural vice, and says to his converts, "Some of you used to be like that; but you have washed it all away, you have become upright, by the power of our Lord Jesus Christ and through the Spirit of our God." (1 Corinthians 6:11, Goodspeed's translation.)

In a later letter he tells them of his experience with what he calls "a thorn in the flesh, a messenger of Satan to harass me." We do not know its nature, though many ingenious conjectures have been made. Some have guessed it was epilepsy, a frequent accompaniment of genius. Whatever it was, it hurt his pride, interfered with his work, gave him this sense of weakness and inferiority of which we have been thinking. "Three times I besought the Lord that it should leave me; but he said to me, 'My grace is sufficient for you, for my power is made perfect in weakness.' Most gladly therefore will I glory in my weakness . . . for when I am weak, then I am strong." (2 Corinthians 12:7-10.)

One of the hardest things for us to learn is that God comes into our lives most readily not at the point of our strength or our success but at the point of our weakness and failure. It is then we own our need of him. Our extremity becomes his opportunity. This is the paradox of Christian experience: "When I am weak, then I am strong." It is then God says to us, "My grace is sufficient for you, for my power is made perfect in weakness." And this is true no matter who we are or what we are or what our past has been or what the future holds.

✠

Prayer

LOOK WITH THY PITY upon us, our Father, weak men and women subsisting under the covert of thy patience but confiding in the promise that thy strength is available to us, thy grace sufficient for us.

Teach us to press our weakness close to thy strength that we may ever know whence to seek and where to find those reserves of power which enable men in every kind of crisis, stress and seeming failure to find the peace of God which passes understanding.

May thy peace guard our hearts and our thoughts in Christ Jesus. Amen.

XI

Kindness Is the Key

THE TWENTY-FIFTH chapter of Matthew, verses 31 to 46, is one of the most important paragraphs in the Bible. It has deeply influenced both theology and art. Its colorful imagery supplied the inspiration for Michelangelo's "The Last Judgment," which some consider the greatest painting in the world. Likewise it inspired Thomas of Celano's "Dies Irae," one of the most celebrated poems of the Middle Ages, which great composers have set to song.

It is not an easy passage to understand. One difficulty appears at the very beginning. Men will be divided at the judgment as the shepherd separates the sheep from the goats. It is a sharp classification which raises more questions than it decides.

Men are not good or bad. They are good and bad, saints and sinners by turn. Syrian sheep were white, Syrian goats were black. They could be easily distinguished, even in the same fold. But men are not all black or white. Some are mottled, some are gray.

Asked a shepherd, "I can see what happens to the sheep and the goats, but what about the alpacas?"—the alpaca being an animal with some of the characteristics of both sheep and goat. Nothing is said of the alpacas. It seems unfair. We might be satisfied with this kind of rough justice if it were meted out in a court of law, for we know how fallible human justice is. We are not satisfied with it as a description of divine justice.

We read on and find it stated that while the righteous enter life eternal, those on the left hand go to eternal punishment: "Depart from me, you cursed, into the eternal fire."

No matter how orthodox their theology or how literal their interpretation of the Bible, few nowadays believe in eternal torment. Said the old Scot when twitted about the article on eternal damnation in his stern Calvinistic creed, "You understand that the Almighty is compelled to do certain things in his official and judicial capacity which he would scorn to do as an individual."

But a God who has to be apologized for is not a God whom we can worship. No matter what the creeds say, few really believe and none wants to believe in eternal damnation. Like Tennyson, we "faintly trust the larger hope."

We know that some get off the course, drift, perhaps make shipwreck, throw away the glorious chance of life which God has given them. We know men and women who are perfectly aware of the difference between right and wrong, who deliberately choose the worst when the best is possible to them. We are almost driven to despair concerning them when we see how through some twist or warp in their nature they defeat every effort to straighten them out. We know men who apparently would rather be dirty than clean, crooked than straight, cruel than kind. Some of them go out of the world with no evidence of repentance.

We are not so superficial, so easygoing in our moral judgments as to think it makes no difference whether a man does right or wrong. Nor does it seem logical to suppose that a man can tread the primrose path to the end, so far as this life is concerned, then do an "about face" at the moment of death.

We believe there is a moral continuum between this life and the next, that there as here we go—as we are told of Judas—to our "own place," the place to which we fit ourselves to go. It is not reasonable to suppose that the universe is so undiscriminating as to lump men together in a common fate, regardless of how they have lived.

Yet when all is said—and I suppose I have seen as many "hopeless cases" as most—I never altogether despair of them. My hope is based on my faith that God is what Jesus says he is, Our Father, and not our father only but the father of all men; that God is like Jesus, that the New Testament is correct in affirming that Jesus truly reveals the character of God. This means that God is better than we are—and none of us would punish a man more or longer than necessary, just to see him squirm. It means not only that God is better than we are; he is better than we dare to dream.

To be sure, we do not know how long the human will is capable of resisting the will of God. We appreciate also the difficulties involved in the idea of conditional immortality, a further probationary period. The Bible and especially the teaching of Jesus lead us to think that the moral choices we make here are decisive. But we believe that God, like the good shepherd in Jesus' story, will seek the lost sheep until he finds it and brings it back to the fold.

The idea of eternal punishment is revolting to our moral sense and a libel on the character of God. Yet here it is, put on the lips of Jesus, and, as Matthew places it, at the very end of the last day of his teaching ministry: "They will go away into eternal punishment, but the righteous into eternal life." With those terrible words Matthew's account of the life of Jesus ends. In the next sentence he begins his narrative of Jesus' death.

What are we to say? Some try to explain or at least soften it by suggesting that the Greek adjective *aionion,* which the versions translate *eternal* or *everlasting,* admits of another meaning. For example, it might mean "spiritual." In John's gospel, eternal life means spiritual life, a matter of quality rather than duration. This explanation is not supported by anyone who knows Greek. I have eight different Greek lexicons in my study. I looked up *aionion* in them all. All agree that it means "eternal," "everlasting." All agree that it refers to duration in time. Greek is a very precise language, much more so than ours. It has an adjective, found often in the New Testament, meaning "spiritual"—the adjective *pneumatikon.* It never uses *aionion* in the sense of *pneumatikon.*

Another explanation involves a knowledge of how the gospels were written. The dates usually given for them are: Mark, about 70; Matthew and Luke, about 85; John, about 100. Assuming that Jesus was crucified in 29 or 30, forty years elapsed before the publication of Mark, the earliest gospel.

The newest school of New Testament criticism, the Formgeshichte school, believes that the gospels are better evidence for Christian preaching and belief at the time they were written, for the faith and practice of the early church, than for the actual words and deeds of Jesus; that we have to go back of the gospels by a process of sifting and comparison to get to the historic Jesus.

The two gospel sources in which scholars have most confidence are Mark, the earliest and briefest of the gospels, based (according to an early and strong tradition which comes to us from Papias, who was Bishop of Hierapolis in Asia Minor about 140, through Eusebius in his church history published about 324) on the reminiscences of Peter and used by both Matthew and Luke as their narrative source; and a collection of the sayings of Jesus, no longer extant, often referred to as "the teaching source," which was earlier than Mark (whether he was familiar with it or not we do not know) and used by both Matthew and Luke, who took Jesus' sayings from it and inserted them into Mark's narrative, Matthew in five big blocks, Luke in smaller sections where he thought them apposite.

In addition, Matthew and Luke had other material peculiar to each. Where they got it we don't know. Perhaps from sources as early and good as Mark and the teaching source. Perhaps from eyewitnesses and earwitnesses of Jesus, for some such would still have been living in Nazareth, in Capernaum and in Jerusalem.

Luke impresses us as a careful and competent historian, a reporter with "a nose for news." In his opening paragraph he describes his sources as "those who from the beginning were eyewitnesses and ministers of the word." It is fascinating to suppose that he got his nativity story from Mary, but it is pure conjecture. He found and incorporated in his gospel a whole cluster of parables found nowhere else. Scholars feel sure of their authenticity, for they bear the unmistakable imprint of Jesus' mind.

About the material peculiar to Matthew, scholars are less sure. I agree with Jülicher that Matthew is "the most important book in the world." But its writer had certain special interests, certain theses to prove—such as that Jesus was the fulfillment of Old Testament prophecy—and these tendencies control his choice of material and his use of it. He had a strong eschatological interest—an interest, that is, in the last things, the end of the age, the final consummation, the judgment, what happens after death. He had apparently been a close student of apocalyptic literature—a type of literature dealing with the end of the age and represented in the Old Testament by the book of Daniel and parts of Ezekiel.

The passage we are studying is found only in Matthew. There is nothing like this dramatic description of the final consummation in any of the other gospels, but close parallels may be found in apocalyptic literature. In the thirty-fourth chapter of Ezekiel, God is represented as a shepherd, judging between sheep and goats. There is nothing in the other gospels corresponding to this scene of the Last Judgment, but the heart of the passage is in these words: "As you did it to one of the least of these my brethren, you did it to me . . . as you did it not to one of the least of these, you did it not to me." (Matthew 25:40, 45.)

To these words there are close parallels elsewhere in the gospels. For example, Mark tells us that Jesus took a child in his arms and set him in the midst of the disciples, who were quarreling about who was the greatest, and said to them, "Whoever receives one such child in my name receives me; . . . Whoever gives a cup of water will by no means lose his reward."

Many scholars feel that the passage in Matthew is part of an early Christian sermon, in which the preacher took this golden saying of Jesus and, in order to give it a vivid, impressive setting, imbedded it in a picturesque judgment scene of the type common in Jewish apocalypse.

If this explanation is correct, then surely we need not take every detail of the passage literally. We can leave the fate of the wicked to a God who is like Jesus and in whose strong hands are the issues of life and death and life to be.

Now forget the framework, the side issue, and concentrate on the main issue. What is the main issue? What is there in the passage which is not taken over from Jewish apocalypse but is new and original and daring? What is it Jesus said that no one else had ever said and no Christian would dare to say if his Master had not said it first? You know without my telling you: that love is the test of discipleship, that our status in the world to which we go will depend on whether we have done the loving thing or left it undone. This is the basic principle by which we are judged.

We know it, yet it involves a reversal of human judgments. It cuts across our usual lines of distinction. Not a man's nationality or the color of his skin. Not his rank or social position. Not the size of his purse nor the titles he is privileged to write before his name nor the degrees he is privileged to write after. But simple, unaffected kindness—feeding the hungry, clothing the naked, being hospitable to the stranger, visiting the sick and the imprisoned. There is nothing dramatic or spectacular about these things. Yet Jesus says they are the important things, the decisive things. Like Wordsworth he regards as

> That best portion of a good man's life:
> His little, nameless, unremembered acts
> Of kindness and of love.

The inference is that this kindness is acceptable even though it lacks the badge of Christian discipleship, that many will discover they are disciples who never regarded themselves as disciples, that there are many unconscious Christians. They do not know they are Christians, yet Christ recognizes them as his. To their surprise they will hear him say, "As you did it to one of the least of these, you did it to me."

Jesus has so identified himself with human need, so bound himself into the bundle of human life, that whoever serves humanity serves him, whoever relieves human need relieves him.

These kindly, generous folk, we are told, were puzzled at the audacity of his statement. "Lord, when did we see thee hungry?" Their kindness had not been done with any sidelong glance for man's approval or praise. It had become the habit of their lives. It was the spontaneous, natural overflow of their hearts.

The others were equally puzzled by their condemnation. They had done nothing wrong. They had never been charged with any crime. They may have been scrupulous in their religious observances, keeping the very letter of the law. Only they were lacking in simple humanity, so self-centered and self-absorbed they were blind to human misery and deaf to human woe. There was no need to pass sentence on them. They passed judgment on themselves.

Love is life, lovelessness its own curse: this is the central impact of our Lord's teaching, the one insistent plea of his life and death, the truth with which his presence forever haunts our earth. We are here for a few years on this giant airship hurtling through the sky. We can jostle our fellow passengers, if we will, elbow them out of the best seats, despise them because their clothes are not cut so well as ours or their grammar is less correct. We can ignore them and seek only our own comfort. Or we can prove ourselves good comrades, remembering him who said, "I have called you friends."

Those who live as friends seem to breathe already the air of that land toward which we are hurrying. With quiet confidence they say, "We know that we have passed out of death into life because we love."

There is deep solemnity in Jesus' statement that this is the only division of men that has eternal significance. He passes by every time-honored standard of value. His basis of judgment is not intellectual nor financial nor even religious in the conventional sense. Men are to be judged simply on the basis of whether or not they have shown themselves human. To those of us who think Jesus knew what he was talking about and meant what he said, these are the most solemn words ever spoken.

In some lectionaries the paragraph we've been studying is appointed to be read during Advent. At first it seems incongruous, but in the light of our study the connection becomes clear: Christ's coming into the world involves judgment.

At Christmastime we like to think of the baby Jesus lying in the manger, wrapped in swaddling clothes, of all that he and his lovely mother have done to soften and regenerate mankind. We must not forget that he is no longer the baby Jesus; he is the king of kings.

We love to linger on the word of the angel to Joseph, "You shall call his name Jesus for he will save his people from their sins." We need to remind ourselves that he came into the world to be not only its saviour but its judge.

His best-loved parables are parables of grace: the Good Samaritan, the lost coin, the lost sheep, the lost son. His most searching parables are parables of judgment, like the two which immediately precede the paragraph we've been studying—the parable of the bridesmaids and the parable of the talents.

You recall the fate of the careless bridesmaids—the door was shut with them on the outside; of the slothful servant—his talent was taken from him and he was cast into the outer darkness. We dare not neglect these sterner aspects of what our Lord's coming means.

Whittier begins his poem "Our Master":

> Immortal Love, forever full,
>   Forever flowing free,
> Forever shared, forever whole,
>   A never-ebbing sea!

He does not end it till he has confessed:

> Thou judgest us; Thy purity
>   Doth all our lusts condemn;
> The love that draws us nearer Thee
>   Is hot with wrath to them.

By our likeness or unlikeness to Jesus we are judged, by whether we reproduce or fail to reproduce his heart of good will. "As you did it to one of the least of these my brethren, you did it to me . . . as you did it not . . . , you did it not to me."

✠

Prayer

We do not pray for things. We pray for some share in the grace of the Lord Jesus Christ, that those we love and those whom we may help and all whose lives touch ours may through us find comfort and joy. Amen.

XII

The Lost Gospel of Jesus

One of the world's most famous and familiar paintings is Da Vinci's "Last Supper." Standing before it, we sense its dramatic power. The souls of the disciples are bared to our gaze in the poignant moment when their Master tells them, "One of you will betray me." We can see the horror and dismay in their faces, almost hear their agonized question, "Is it I, Lord?"

The second impression is one of disappointment as we look at the central figure. Peter, Matthew, James, John—in them we see the lineaments of strong men in the grip of strong emotion. But the face of Jesus is colorless, passionless, effeminate, sad. We ask ourselves, How could such an insipid person command the loyalty of such virile men? Can this be he who said, "I came to cast fire upon the earth: would that it were already kindled!"?

When we turn from the conventional pictures of Jesus to the Jesus of the gospels we find a convincing negative answer. Even a cursory examination reveals a dynamic personality, physically robust—or he could not have trudged the hot and dusty roads of Palestine on his preaching tours; mentally keen and alert, so that his opponents engaged in debate with him to their own discomfiture; with a sanity, reserve and poise found only in the strongest; who taught with authority; who drew strong men to him and whose first words to them were, "Follow me."

Here is no pale Galilean, no wan ascetic, no idle dreamer, no stained-glass saint, but a vigorous and forceful figure who might well say, "I came to cast fire upon the earth," for he kindled in men's hearts a holy flame which the gusts of the centuries have not extinguished.

The prologue to the Fourth Gospel speaks sober truth: "In him was life, and the life was the light of men. Amid the darkness the light still shines, for the darkness has never put it out." Tender and gentle he was, but without softness and sentimentality, the tenderness often found in a rugged and masculine nature.

"You know the grace of our Lord Jesus," says Paul, as though it were something everyone knew; from the Greek word which our versions translate *grace* comes our word *charm*. Charming and gracious, with a surpassing courtesy which made no distinction between high and low, rich and poor, yet with a spiritual detachment no circumstance could break.

To know him calls for imaginative sympathy rather than technical scholarship. In his teaching we find no such carefully worked-out system of thought as we find in Aristotle's *Nichomachean Ethics* or Calvin's *Institutes* or Herbert Spencer's *Synthetic Philosophy*. We find flashes of insight called forth by a specific situation—the spontaneous expression of a varied and vital spiritual experience—rather than sustained and systematic thought; a poetic sensitiveness and a prophetic passion rather than critical acumen and philosophical subtlety. Love rather than logic is the key to an understanding of Jesus.

In him conviction and conduct, creed and character, are one. The open secret of his personality is to be found in three dominant convictions he wholly believed and wholly lived. To them he gave his single-minded devotion. For them he gave his life. To face them will search us through and through, for they are so revolutionary, so contrary to established ideas, that his disciples in all ages have quailed before their implications and taken refuge in the comfortable respectability which often masquerades as Christianity. In the haunting words of H. G. Wells, "To this day the Galilean is too great for our small hearts." What are these convictions? Although, as we have noted, he did not put his teaching in systematic form, it is possible to reduce to three items the essentials of his creed.

The Reality of God

God is the center of every high form of religion. The poets and prophets of Israel had set forth the holiness of God in lofty and moving words. As Jesus learned the Shema (Deuteronomy 6:4, 5) at his mother's knee, he caught his first glimpse of the Holy One of Israel. In these hidden years his inherited faith became a personal experience. All nature was to him a disclosure of God, who reveals his beauty in sunset and dawn, flower and star.

Over all human life broods a wise and loving Father. How meaningful the word *Father* becomes in the matchless story beginning, "There was a man who had two sons."

As Jesus tells us about the Father, we are astonished and

incredulous—it seems too good to be true. He knows us. Despite the vast number living today, the vaster number who have lived here in the past, he knows us every one. With Oriental hyperbole, Jesus says he knows the number of hairs in our heads—a picturesque way of saying that his knowledge runs beyond our boldest imagination. He cares for us. In spite of accident, calamity, the vicissitude of circumstance, the caprice of fate, he cares for us every one. He loves us. Despite our folly and our sin, he loves us every one. He forgives us. No matter how far we have wandered or how long we have sinned, he waits to welcome us as soon as we say, "I will arise and go to my Father."

He suffers with us and for us—that incredible truth the cross reveals. He needs us—for the need of the companionship of his children is the essence of fatherhood. So amazing is Jesus' disclosure of God's fatherhood that men have never quite dared to believe it.

But the originality and power of Jesus lie not so much in what he tells us of God as in his own experience of God. How constantly he drew upon it, his every word and work reveal. It was an undying fire that even death could not put out.

It is different with us. I wonder whether God's presence was ever farther from men's consciousness than now. Some tell you with a shrug, some with the sadness of regret how God has slipped out of their lives. Just as Einstein's formulae are meaningless to one who knows nothing of physics and mathematics, so Jesus' language concerning God is largely unintelligible to us because of our spiritual ignorance, our absorption in material things. The spirit of the time denies God's holiness by its irreverence; by its skepticism and cynicism, his love.

Yet he who listens to the undertones of modern life knows that this clever, brittle, erotic, neurotic, feverish, fear-ridden, pleasure-mad age has a strange wistfulness for the unseen and eternal, is unsatisfied by the tinsel glitter of the world's Vanity Fair, ever and again echoes Job's cry, "O, that I knew where I might find him!"

In this inarticulate, largely unconfessed longing lies the church's opportunity. The open door of the church is an avenue into the presence of God. The entire service from introit to benediction should have as its aim to make God's presence real, to help men feel that this is the house of God, where they can meet him if they will.

Worship is the distinctive function of the church. It does other good things, has other valuable activities, but—with the exception of the religious training of the young and the promotion of the missionary enterprise—everything else the church does other agencies also are doing. Nowhere else do men gather in answer to the call, "O come, let us worship and bow down; let us kneel before the Lord, our Maker!" The first business of the church is to realize Jesus' experience of God and then impart it to a restless, needy world.

The Worth of the Human Soul

Since time began, men have sought for something holy as a focus of devotion: shrines, temples, altars, sacraments, sacred days. Jesus found the temple of God in a most unlikely place: the human soul. The divinest thing in the world was a human being. He took children in his arms and said, "Of such is the kingdom of God."

He had a sublime faith in the possibilities of human nature, was sure that even the most degraded and unlovely member of the human family was a child of God.

Man's life on earth was not to Jesus a vale of tears between two eternities. He dignified and exalted it, characterized it as "eternal," by which he meant not duration but quality. Life here and now may be so rich in eternal values that it can never cease. This teaching of Jesus is our one sure hope of immortality. "This is life eternal, to know God": the eternal life he knew from his own communion with God he offers to share with us.

The method of Jesus' ministry was shaped by his conviction of the worth of the individual soul. He never sought the crowd. The crowd sought him. He sought the individual, especially the one whom others overlooked. The man nobody saw was the man he saw. The man others neglected was the man he sought out. Much of his most important teaching was given not to a large congregation but to twelve men or to two or three or to a single person, like Nicodemus or the woman he met at Jacob's well. He trusted the future not to an elaborate program or organization but to a handful of men, sure that their faith would be kindled by his and in turn light the flame of faith in others.

Today we live in an era of organization, of mass production and mass movements, with a mechanistic philosophy and a passion for conferences and conventions, programs and surveys. The individual is dwarfed by the vastness and complexity of the universe the new telescopes reveal—"astronomically intimidated," as someone has said—and by an increasing tendency toward standardization that reduces all men to the level of the mass.

The state asserts itself against the individual, the individual is lost in the state. In a totalitarian state, the state is deified; the doctrine frankly preached that the state is everything, the individual nothing. He has no rights, no liberties not conferred by the state. As the state gave them, the state can take them away. We have not reached that point in America. We still hold with the great declaration that men are endowed by their Creator (not by the state) with certain unalienable rights; that among these are life, liberty and the pursuit of happiness; that to secure these governments are instituted among men, deriving their just powers from the consent of the governed; in short, that government is made for man, not the other way around.

But we no longer hold to the idea that that government is best which rests most lightly on its citizens. I am not competent to appraise the paternalistic state, the welfare state, to balance its benefits against its drawbacks. I simply make the point that as the state becomes stronger and takes to itself more functions, the individual more and more feels himself a pawn on the chessboard, moved this way or that by forces he cannot control.

Modern industry tends to dwarf the individual. No good to inveigh against the factory system. It has given us a higher standard of living than men ever had before. But thoughtful employers are concerned over the effect of large-scale, assembly-line production on the worker who—if he thinks at all as he stands all day performing a repetitive operation—must think of himself as a cog in the wheel, an appendage to the machine he serves.

A college contemporary of mine inherited a shoe factory. The business was started by his grandfather who made shoes by hand. As his business grew he employed men and taught them the trade. "People can't afford custom shoes today," says my friend, "the cost is prohibitive. And machine-made shoes wear as well. But as I watch my employees stamping out soles and heels, I know they don't get as much fun out of their work as my grandfather got out of his."

One Sunday I preached in Youngstown. The man who drove me to the station said, "You've half an hour till train-time. Would you like to see the city?" So he showed me the huge plant of Youngstown Sheet and Tube, sprawling along the Mahoning Valley for a mile or more. This is the age of steel. Steelmaking is a modern miracle, the basis of our material civilization. But how can men as they pour through the gates of these Gargantuan steel mills when the whistle blows feel themselves anything but cogs in the machine?

If thoughtful employers are concerned about this aspect of industrialism, thoughtful labor leaders may well be too. How can a man in a big union—the largest, the United Automobile Workers, has a million members; the United Steel Workers almost as many—feel himself anything but a pawn in a game which is played at union headquarters in Detroit or Pittsburgh or Washington?

The spirit of the age has laid its spell even on the church, turning its attention from the individual to mass movements, organizations, drives directed from denominational headquarters where the plans are made and handed down to the local church. Our assemblies are overloaded with business, weak in inspiration, dominated by the ecclesiastical machine. In our cities the church has become a larger unit than in the past. This makes possible a trained staff, a diversified program with ample talent to carry it on, the enthusiasm engendered by an organization of striking power. But again the individual is in danger of being lost.

You cannot keep a live church from growing larger, for—unlike a club of limited membership—it is a church's business to project itself on the community, to reach all the people it can. Perhaps a solution is to break the membership down into small groups or cells for fellowship, spiritual discipline and culture, in line with a suggestion made by Elton Trueblood in his thoughtful book, *Alternative to Futility*.

At least in our worship we can help the individual to remember that the primary relationship is between God and his soul. We can turn our backs on impersonal mass methods of winning men and recover the personal method of Jesus. "One loving heart sets another on fire": so an early Christian described it. It accounts for the amazing spread of the new religion in its early days.

The Coming of God's Kingdom

If you had never seen a New Testament and I put one in your hand and said, "Read the first three gospels and tell me what is the central idea in Jesus' teaching," you would turn the pages and say, "He is always talking about the kingdom of God. It runs through all his teaching and gives it a kind of unity."

It is the dominant theme of his parables. How many of them begin, "The kingdom of God is like," as by simile and paradox he sought to make it vivid and clear! To it he gave his utter allegiance, for it he died. It was the vision in his own soul of the reign of God in human life when his will is done on earth "till earth shall shine among the stars, its sins wiped out, its captives free"—the most magnificent, challenging, revolutionary idea that ever entered the human mind. It filled his mind with a divine fire that flames through his words and deeds. The passion with which he proclaimed it so startled the ruling classes of his day that they felt they had to get rid of him lest the established order which had brought them power and privilege should be overthrown.

The idea of the kingdom did not originate with Jesus. It had a long history behind it. It is found in the prophets and in the later writers who wrote during the centuries which intervene between the close of the Old Testament canon and the beginning of the New.

Many of the prophetic writings come from the time of the exile. It was then men dreamed of a day when God would establish his kingdom on the earth, for—as is natural to our resilient human nature—when times are darkest, hope shines brightest. When the exile was over and the people restored to their land, a day would dawn when God would reign supreme, when there would be one faith throughout the earth, when war would be no more, the weapons of war transformed into implements of peace, when nature would glow with enhanced beauty, the sun be seven times brighter, when the wild beasts would lose their fierceness, the lion lie down with the lamb.

These idyllic pictures charmed and solaced the people's minds during the long exile, but when after seventy years they returned to their own land they felt let down. Those who returned had never known what it was to be free or to rule themselves. They did not know how to use their freedom. They were torn by dissension. Their weakness brought first the Greeks and then the Romans upon them. Their holy city was occupied by foreign troops. A mood of pessimism settled upon them. They did not lose their expectation of a coming day of the Lord, but it took a more somber form. The teachers who now arose spoke as if the world were so bad it could not be reformed from within. But when it got bad enough, God would break in suddenly from without with flaming authority and rending cataclysm, trample his enemies underfoot, take his power and reign. In this dramatic fashion would his kingdom come.

When Jesus began to teach, men wanted to know what he had to say about the kingdom. "You do not have to wait for it," he said, "it is here. It is among you. It is within you." Everything his eyes fell upon, he said, "The kingdom of God is like that." If he saw a farmer sowing his fields, he said, "The kingdom of God is like that." If he saw fishermen pulling in their nets, he said, "The kingdom is like that." If he saw a housewife making bread, he said, "The kingdom is like that: like the yeast which works silently, unobtrusively, pervasively until it leavens the whole loaf. You do not have to wait for some catastrophic incursion of divine power from without: the kingdom is here."

He was not blind to evil, none more aware than he of its presence and its malignant power. But the kingdom would come in spite of it. A sower goes forth to sow. Some of the seed falls on the wayside and birds devour it, some on shallow soil where it cannot root, some among thorns where it is choked out. But some falls on good ground and bears abundant fruit.

The kingdom is like a man who sowed good seed, but an enemy sowed tares among his wheat. His servants asked if they should pull up the tares. He answered, "Let both grow together until the harvest." Evil will be present until the end. But the kingdom is not defeated because tares grow amid the wheat. The wheat is growing too. All a man has to do is open his heart to God, live in harmonious relation with him. The kingdom of God is here.

No thoughtful man can long forget the background of world tragedy against which we live our lives, the fear, distress, despair of which the world is full. Nevertheless, the kingdom is here. The reason for the chaos is that men have not lived as though they were citizens of God's eternal kingdom of righteousness, peace and joy. They have lived as though this earth were a jungle of wild beasts. They have never given themselves to the discovery of moral dynamics with the same earnestness that they have given themselves to the discovery of material wealth, never really believed in moral power as they have believed in physical power.

When Napoleon cynically declared that God is on the side of the heavier battalions, when Stalin asked ironically, "The Pope? How many divisions has the Pope?" they were expressing the idea of power which men of power, as this world appraises power, have always held.

Yet Jesus says, "The kingdom of God is like treasure hidden in a field, which a man found and in his joy sold all that he had and bought that field . . . like a merchant in search of fine pearls who, finding one pearl of great value, sold all he had and bought it." It is a test, a touchstone, a constant challenge to heroism and to faith.

It is like your business. "What," you ask, "do you preachers in your ivory towers know about business with its labor trouble, its governmental regulation, its cutthroat competition, its getting contracts not by the quality of one's product but by knowing the right people, people whose influence is for sale?"

That is where the test comes. You may have started out on your business career with high ideals, but when pressure was put on you, you succumbed, saying, "Business is business," and now the kingdom to you is a vague memory of bygone dreams. You should have sold all you had to be true to it. Business itself is only possible in the long run on the principles of the kingdom, such as, "Whatever you wish that men would do to you, do so to them."

If you let go your moral restraint, do business not like a citizen of God's kingdom but like a beast of prey, you are doing what if everyone did it would put an end to business. The kingdom is no cheap and easy thing. Jesus never said it was. What he said was "It is here. If men are big enough, brave enough, patient enough, persistent enough, constructive enough, they can enter it, become citizens of it now."

This is the lost gospel of Jesus. Almost before his voice was stilled his central emphasis had begun to disappear. The phrase "kingdom of God"—with Matthew's synonym "kingdom of heaven"—occurs 135 times in the gospels (some of these are duplicates), thirteen times in the epistles. In the Revelation it has become a mystic symbol. Before the first century passed it had vanished from sight. You search for it in vain through the writings of the church fathers, through the creeds, hymns, liturgies of the succeeding centuries. Is not this the strangest fact of Christian history that the master idea of Jesus which he made the goal of his life, of all human aspiration and endeavor, has been ignored by Christianity; that what meant everything to him has meant nothing to his church?

The gospel of the kingdom has been rediscovered in our day. Many of our leaders have caught Jesus' vision of a redeemed world as the goal of Christian effort and the mission of the church. But the world wants none of it. It is too revolutionary, too disturbing. The ruling forces of our day, like the ruling forces of Jesus' day, want no such radical ideas. Such a gospel is impractical. It does not fit modern conditions.

Modern civilization could not have been built on the basis of the Sermon on the Mount. But as Dr. Walter Russell Bowie says, "Perhaps modern civilization could not have been built on Jesus' teaching, but what could be built upon it is something far better than modern civilization." Our missionaries are constantly embarrassed and impeded by the patent fact, which the so-called heathen perceives with disconcerting clearness, that Christianity is not Christian. The truth is that we must Christianize America before we can evangelize the world; and to do this we must believe and proclaim Jesus' gospel of the kingdom.

Only so can the church regain its moral leadership. It is not hated and persecuted today as it was in the days of Nero and Caligula, but it is not respected. It does a lot of unadvertised good. But its hesitancy and timidity, its silence and inaction in face of moral issues have forfeited men's respect. Its tepid, conventional ways are a long way from him who said, "I came to cast fire upon the earth: would that it were already kindled!"

Let us be under no illusion as to what will happen if the church boldly proclaims the gospel of the kingdom and begins in earnest to apply it. It will meet opposition. Mammonism, materialism and militarism: these were the forces that nailed Jesus to the cross because his gospel of the kingdom ran counter to them. They are still with us. Yet nothing less does he expect of us. This Carpenter of Nazareth expects his church to stand for social justice. This Prince of Peace expects his church to spearhead the attack on war.

He is not so impractical as practical men think. He did build a kingdom which has outlasted the kingdoms of this world, which is here for those who will live as its citizens. We have had enough disappointments to know how far it is from being fully realized. But it makes a difference when a man sees that this world belongs to God, that all that is wrong with it is that we are not clean enough, brave enough, unselfish enough to co-operate with him in bringing in his kingdom.

The Threefold Faith

Faith in God, faith in man, faith in the coming of his kingdom: so simply may we state the creed of Jesus. He summons us not so much to believe in him as to believe with him, not so much to confess him as to incarnate him, not so much to reverence his character as to reproduce it. Searching, commanding, thrilling, may these three convictions become ours, that we may truly be his disciples, sharing his passion and his power.

✠

Prayer

O CHRIST, whose name we so often take upon our lips but whose presence and power we so seldom feel in our lives, make thyself real to us, that we may commit ourselves anew to thee, that thy creed may be our creed, thy convictions our convictions, that we may think and will and do what they must think and will and do who take thee seriously. Amen.

XIII

The Halo on Life

To the student of psychology (which includes almost all of us in greater or less degree), nothing is more fascinating than dreams. One of the best books on the subject is Havelock Ellis' *The World of Dreams.* Since its publication in 1911 it has been overshadowed by the more popular writings of the Freudian school: Dr. Sigmund Freud, who, however subject to modification his findings are, must be counted one of the most brilliant and influential thinkers of our time; and his eminent disciples, who differed with him at some points but used his method, Doctors Brill, Adler and Jung. Havelock Ellis uses the biological approach, the Freudians that of clinical experience.

The Freudians in particular attach the utmost importance to dreams, believing that by means of them they can interpret our repressed desires—the urges and conflicts which during our waking hours we keep imprisoned in the abysmal region below the level of consciousness but, when we are asleep and the sentinel is off guard, force their way up and out in the form of dreams.

In Bible times also men were keenly interested in dreams, attaching great significance to them. Jacob, Joseph, Ezekiel, Daniel—what dreamers they were! When from the Old

Testament we turn to the New, we find it closes with a dream dreamed by an exile on an island in the Aegean Sea.

In the tenth chapter of Acts we are told of a man who had a curious dream and on awaking assumed that through it God had spoken to him, telling him something he wanted him to know. For there is this difference between the Biblical interpretation of dreams and the Freudian: the latter connects them with our own subconscious desires, the former connects them with God.

This man had gone up on a housetop to pray. It was noon and he was hungry. While lunch was being prepared he fell into a trance. He saw the heaven open and a huge sheet, containing all manner of animals and reptiles, lowered by its four corners to the ground. A voice came to him: "Rise, Peter; kill and eat." He answered, "No, Lord; for I have never eaten anything that is common or unclean." Again the voice came: "What God has cleansed, you must not call common."

What Dr. Freud and his confreres would make of that I do not know, though I fear those animals and reptiles would put Peter in a bad light. But this is how Peter interpreted it in the light of what followed: "God has shown me that I should not call any man common or unclean."

Note that verb, *shown*. It recalls an old but pungent slang phrase, "I've got to be shown"; "You've got to show me." Here was a man who had to be shown. I think we all, even the most self-willed and self-sufficient of us, feel the need of that, especially in face of life's shadowed experiences—pain, trouble, loneliness, temptation, death. We want to be shown their meaning.

We feel we can bear whatever we have to bear if we can

see that these shadowed experiences have meaning, are not simply fate's caprice. We want someone to interpret their meaning to us. So we come to church, as the pilgrim came to the Interpreter's House in Bunyan's tale, that we may have light thrown on the mysteries that surround us, the dark and puzzling experiences through which we have to go.

Perhaps someone asks, "Why do we need to be shown? Why not go our own way, pick our own path?" In the fifteenth chapter of Luke we find the story of a young man who said and did precisely that, who came at last to the husks and the swine, a sadder and a wiser man. And when he came to himself he said, "I will arise and go to my father." How many of us can make John Henry Newman's prayer our own?

> I was not ever thus, nor prayed that thou
>   Shouldst lead me on;
> I loved to choose and see my path; but now
>   Lead thou me on!
> I loved the garish day, and, spite of fears,
> Pride ruled my will: remember not past years.

Those of us who have stumbled and fallen know our insufficiency, our need of someone to show us the way.

This man believed he had found someone: "God has shown me." What does that mean? It means that at the heart of every experience, however baffling and mysterious, there is an unseen Presence to show us the meaning of it, to illumine the path where our next step will fall, to hold us up, to guide us through. This in a sentence is the religious interpretation of life. In this conviction religious men of all ages and whatever creed are one.

What did God show him? "God has shown me that I should not call any man common or unclean." In other words, God showed him the halo which is on all of life, if we have eyes to see. Peter with his rigid Jewish outlook needed to be shown that.

And so do we. For many of our popular writers, whom I shall not name because I do not intend to advertise their books, seem engaged in a conspiracy to knock the halo off. Much of our current fiction and drama is a combination of moral cynicism and sheer nastiness, where men and women are depicted as the sport of their vagrant passions and untamed desires.

Their authors seem to glory in this reversion to primitivism, uncaring of the generations of struggle and restraint by which our dear-bought civilization has been won. War always brings an inflation of currency and a deflation of moral standards, a coarsening of manners, speech and conduct. Anyone to whom refinement of soul is an ideal is deemed a hypocrite or a prig.

Do you recall in *Les Miserables* how Jean Valjean carries Marius through the sewers of Paris? It wasn't their fault that they were down there amid the darkness and filth. But the pity of it was that above them was the most beautiful city in the world and that there are more pleasant ways of reaching the Seine River and the ocean beyond than via the sewer route.

Certainly the sewer is one aspect of reality, a necessary adjunct to urban life. I believe in sewers, but I believe they should be kept in their proper place—underground, out of sight. I do not care to have them flowing across my library table. We have a considerable number of sewer novelists, sewer playwrights, sewer psychologists, who make their gains by exposing the sordid side of human nature, pandering to their fellows' morbid curiosity. I shall not be so prudish or dishonest as to pretend I have not read some of them. Like everyone else, I fatuously imagine that however such books may harm others they can't harm a sophisticated man of the world like me, who has standards against which to judge them. But as one grows older and feels the pressure of the years and is increasingly conscious of eyestrain, he begins to wonder how much time he can wisely spend on reading of this type.

"Don't you know," asks Goethe, "that if you read this you can't read that?" Once I asked a friend if he had read a sensational "best seller." "No," said he, "I'm sixty. When a man reaches the point where he knows he has only five or ten working years left, he realizes he can't read everything, he's got to pick and choose."

"The older I get," declared Emerson, "the more easily I content myself with the great books: Shakespeare, Milton, the Bible."

The halo on life: have you ever noticed how the best writers show it to us, often where we should least expect to find it? Dickens shows us treasures of affection and character in the London slums. Hugo does the same for the slums of Paris. Kipling shows us the generous and loyal camaraderie of the barrack room and lonely garrison. Browning in "Pippa Passes" shows us the charm and influence of a little factory girl, rejoicing in her one holiday of the year. Burns shows us the beauty of a mountain daisy uprooted by a plow, the pathos of a field mouse whose nest has been destroyed. Again he glorifies family life in a humble home in

"The Cotter's Saturday Night" as Whittier does in "Snowbound."

Have you ever studied Millet's familiar painting, "The Angelus"? Two people stand in a field at close of day as a distant church bell tolls the hour of prayer. One is a maiden who devoutly bows her head and clasps her hands. The other is a young man who stands fumbling with his hat and looking a trifle foolish. Beside them is a wheelbarrow containing the tools they have been using.

The high spot of the picture is formed by the rays of the setting sun. Do you remember on what Millet makes those rays fall? If you or I had been painting the picture, we should probably have let them fall on the girl's reverently bowed head or folded hands. Not so Millet. He lets them fall on the wheelbarrow and the tools. It is a great artist's tribute to the dignity of the common task. He shows us the halo on the lowliest toil.

Is not this the supreme service these God-illumined seers do us? They show us the sacramental meaning of the common task and the common day.

Emerson speaks for them all when he says:

> 'Tis not in the high stars alone,
> Nor in the redbreast's mellow tone,
> But in the mud and scum of things,
> There always, always something sings.

The man of religion, like the artist and the poet, looks for the something that sings, the reflection in human life of the God in whose image and by whose creative love it was made, the God who is ever showing us—if we have ears to hear and eyes to see—that we should not call any man common or unclean.

But it is supremely in the man Christ Jesus that God has shown us that human life is not common but a high and holy thing. Because his feet walked its common ways this earth is forever hallowed. His hands were calloused with its rough, hard toil and therefore every man who does his share of the world's hard work may feel a sense of high vocation. He thought through a human brain, and so we know our brains were given us to think thoughts not only of having and holding, getting and spending, but of truth and beauty, duty and destiny, immortality and God:

> Strange that we creatures of the petty ways,
> Poor prisoners behind these fleshly bars,
> Can sometimes think us thoughts with God ablaze,
> Touching the fringes of the outer stars.

His radiant spirit clothed itself in a human body, expressed itself through a human body; so we know these bodies of ours, which often seem so carnal and gross, so of the earth earthy, are to be made the outward and visible sign of an inner and spiritual grace.

We know that men are selfish, lazy, stupid, sometimes malignant and cruel—we don't need anyone to show us that. There are moods when we are tempted to speak of them, as Carlyle did of the inhabitants of Britain, as "mostly fools"; to define the *genus homo* as Mencken did—"a cross between a jackal and a jackass." We believe in the divine capacities of men, not chiefly because of what we see in our fellows or ourselves but because once in history a plain man, a carpenter in an obscure village, embodied the fullness of God, and because we believe that in him all men—the last, the least, the lowest—may be made complete. The Man of Nazareth has shown us that we should not call any man common or unclean.

It is a serious thing when we allow ourselves to fall into a mood of cynicism and disparagement where we lose sight of the halo on life, a serious thing for a Christian when he finds it easier to despise than to admire. If you are cherishing low views of life, unable to see anything in your fellows but what is cheap and contemptible and vile, look at him who took upon himself our manhood and so made manhood holy forevermore.

If it is a serious matter to cherish low views of others it is even more serious to think in low terms of oneself. I do not know how you are thinking of yourself. Perhaps you have that sense of futility and defeat we call an inferiority complex. Perhaps you are saying to yourself, "What a poor, second-rate specimen I am, so whipped and beaten, so devoid of self-confidence and self-control. What did God have in mind when he made me?"

So you may be thinking of yourself. Not so is he thinking of you. Over every one of us his spirit broods. To every soul he whispers, "What fine possibilities you have, if you will let me help you bring them to the light!"

You, with all the marks of your brute inheritance upon you, are made in the likeness of God, entrusted with powers that will go on unfolding through the ages, fitted for communion with him, with a spirit as eternal as his own. He has set eternity in our hearts, that short of him we should ne'er be satisfied. He has put his seal upon us, claiming each one for his own. This is the gospel I bring you. Believe it, for it is true. In Jesus—the one altogether beautiful, the infinitely fair—God has shown us that we should not call any man common or unclean.

Prayer

HERE THOU SEEST, O Lord, all sorts and conditions of men: youth with its troubled dreams or savage cynicism, mid-life with its faded idealism or hard realism, age with its prophetic faith or dull, gray resignation. Some of us have won success and are tempted to pride; some have met with failure and are tempted to despair. All types of mind, all degrees of culture and development, pilgrims at every stage of the journey, we come here to rest our souls on thee, to raise our pilgrim song ere we resume our climbing way.

We bless thee that while our love for thee has tides that ebb and flow, thy love for us is ever at the full; that though in our varied preoccupations we often forget thee, the Lord is mindful of his own, he remembereth his children. We thank thee for the faith that keeps us faithful to the highest we know, so that we cannot long rest in any easy second-best, but however often we falter and fall must arise to renew our ever-failing but never-ceasing quest of perfection. We thank thee that we can admire moral beauty in others, can rejoice in the joys of others with spirits envy-free.

Forgive us our base ingratitude, our smug acceptance of

thy gifts as though they were ours of right and not of grace; our weak amiability, which is often another name for moral cowardice; our attitude of fatalism toward our own besetting sins; our uncharitableness toward the sins of others; the false and easy optimism which leads us to assume we can correct our faults any time and so keeps us from trying to correct them today. Forgive us the low hankerings we can hardly forgive ourselves.

Give to each one the gift of thy grace he most needs: healing to those who are hurt, light to those in darkness, comfort to the lonely and sad, courage and strength to us all. Teach us how to live, how to love, how to hope, despite the tramp of the heavy years.

Our Master, once more we make thy faith our prayer: "Thy Kingdom come! Thy will be done on earth!" Amen.

XIV

The Risks of Prayer

THOSE who are wise in spiritual things have always recognized that the inner core of religion is prayer, the practice of the presence of God. Said Novalis, "Prayer makes religion real." Said Baron von Hügel, "Prayer is to religion what thought is to philosophy." Said James Martineau, "The generations may perish; but between the spirit of man and the Spirit of God the relation is steady and eternal—an asking from below, a benediction from above." Communion with the infinite and eternal Spirit to whom our spirits are akin is the highest act of which man is capable.

Teachers of religion do what they can to encourage people to cultivate the life of prayer. In my communicant class I spend an hour in discussing the elements of prayer—adoration, thanksgiving, confession, petition and intercession—and in giving practical suggestions on how to pray.

There is one aspect of prayer of which preachers seldom speak, though to be completely honest they should: the risks of prayer. Prayer may be associated in your mind with comfort, peace, assurance, repose. In a tumultuous world, multitudes find these benisons in prayer as nowhere else.

> Thou Life within my life, than self more near,
> Thou veiled Presence infinitely clear,
> From all illusive shows of sense I flee,
> To find my center and my rest in thee.

Yet I should not be your friend if I did not warn you that prayer also exposes those who engage in it to serious risks.

The first is the risk of *seeing ourselves as we are*. "Know thyself" were the words graven over the entrance of the temple of Delphi, words first attributed to one of the seven sages, Solon of Athens, who lived in the seventh century B.C. It is not easy to know ourselves, nor is it entirely pleasant. He who would know himself must be willing to face himself, hard as this sometimes turns out to be. Without becoming morbidly introspective, he must ask himself: What are my motives, my dominant desires? What do I want above everything else? What kind of thoughts do I most frequently entertain when alone? What is my attitude toward other people? What are my talents? Am I using them for good ends? What are my weaknesses? Am I trying to overcome them? Do I judge myself by the standard of those about me, content if I am doing no worse than they, or do I judge myself by an ideal standard, the standard of the best I know?

What we think of ourselves is often what we want to be thought rather than what we are. The dodges of self-deception are legion—the devices we use to escape from telling ourselves the truth about ourselves. We are reluctant to acknowledge our moral failures and accept responsibility for them.

Once I talked with a man about a motor accident in which he was involved, to which there were no witnesses. Said he,

"It was my fault. I turned off the road without seeing the other car." The habit of honesty was ingrained in him, which was why people trusted him; but how often have you heard a man admit that in a motor accident the fault was his? If we are loath to acknowledge our mistakes, how much more our moral failures!

It is an axiom with psychologists that we tend to repress anything which conflicts with our self-love, our self-esteem, because it is painful to us. Hence we turn a blind eye to our faults and salve our conscience by the familiar devices known as rationalization and projection.

Rationalization is the process of giving ourselves plausible excuses for doing what we have already done or made up our minds to do. Projection is the procedure whereby we condemn our own faults in others. We parents are likely to be harsh in dealing with our own faults when we see them cropping out in our children. It is really self-condemnation, but we do not recognize it as such.

Not only are we blind to our defects, but the situation is further complicated by our faculty for seeing virtues in ourselves which are not there. Like Mr. Mitty in James Thurber's classic tale, we indulge in fantasies, reveries, daydreaming, wish-thinking; we picture ourselves as heroes, martyrs, philanthropists. We harbor the notion that by our families and fellow workers we are unappreciated and misunderstood.

It is possible that we may go on to the end of our days still cherishing our illusions, our self-fantasy; but if anything happens to strip us of our illusions, force us to face the truth about ourselves, it is likely to make us desperately unhappy. It would be interesting to know how many nervous breakdowns are the result of the victims' being forced to face the truth about themselves.

This is why prayer is a healthful if humbling practice. In prayer we voluntarily face the truth about ourselves. We know how unavailing are pose and pretense in our relation with him "to whom [in the solemn words of the communion collect] all hearts are open, all desires known and from whom no secrets are hid."

The man who tries to be evasive in prayer is as silly as the misguided folk who consult a doctor to find out what is wrong with them, have him prescribe a regimen for improving their health but don't tell him the whole truth about themselves; then think it smart to cheat a little on the regimen he prescribes by taking an occasional highball or an occasional whipped-cream dessert.

If you expect a doctor to help you, you have to come clean. In our dealings with God we have to come clean. All our subterfuges, the flimsy excuses we contrive to hide our inner poverty from ourselves, must come down. We face the truth about ourselves when we ask God to take us as we are and make us as we ought to be. It is the prerequisite to moral progress, but it is hard on our pride.

The second risk of prayer is the danger of *becoming more like Jesus* in a world which crucified him and would do it again. The deity we Americans more than any other people secretly worship is the one Carlyle described as "the bitch-goddess success."

Recently an enterprising publisher reprinted four of the novels of Horatio Alger, Jr. Horatio Alger, Jr., is only a name to the boys of today, but he was as well known in my boyhood as Superman and Tarzan are to the boys of today. Thousands of American boys born between 1870 and 1910 pictured themselves as Alger heroes. His books were in all our bookcases, were frequently given as prizes in Sunday schools. He wrote 130 of them, but they were not 130 different stories; they were 130 versions of the same story under different titles such as *Struggling Upward, Pluck and Luck, Plan and Prosper, Work and Win.*

In every one the hero begins as Ragged Dick the Bootblack, and by patient, plodding merit becomes Richard the Merchant Prince; or he begins as Tom the Train Boy and ends as president of the road. They are highly moral books in the sense that they contain no bad words and their heroes are paragons of virtue, polite, cheerful, ambitious, industrious, on the make. They are highly immoral books in representing virtue as invariably leading to worldly success. It doesn't.

There is nothing reprehensible about success. The fact that a man is successful doesn't prove him a rogue any more than the fact he is a failure proves him a saint. The qualities that produce success are often admirable qualities. Failure is often due to indolence or stupidity. But there come times in the life of every man when he has to choose between doing the clever thing, the advantageous thing, or the right thing, and, if he chooses the right thing, taking the consequences.

Jesus was faced by this choice at the outset of his career. He must have told his disciples about it, for they could have learned of it in no other way; and in typical Hebraic fashion he objectified and dramatized an inner experience. The tempter came to him with three temptations which had this in common: all three were temptations to use his unique personal power in such a way as to win worldly success. Who can doubt but that with his unique personal power he could have had anything he wanted in the way of worldly success? The temptation that came to him at the beginning of his ministry may have returned many times during it, for Luke tells us significantly that the tempter "departed from him for a season."

We do not know how severe his struggle was, for we have never been subjected to temptation on the same scale. We do know that he always saw it as a temptation, always conquered it, always chose not to be smart but to be right. His integrity brought him not fame and fortune but loneliness and a felon's death. He foresaw his impending fate. He shrank from it as any normal, healthy man in his early thirties would. He prayed in agony to be delivered from it. He had to screw his courage to the sticking place to go through with it. But when it came to a choice between going back on his ideals and winning what the world calls success or being true to his ideals and taking the consequence in ignominious failure, his choice was made.

When we pray, we pray God to show us what is right, to give us ethical discernment, and then the strength of purpose to do what is right. We Christians offer that prayer in Jesus' name. A second risk of prayer is the danger of becoming more like Jesus in a world which crucified him and would crucify him again.

A third risk is closely related to the second: the danger of *having our prayer answered*. Do you believe God answers prayer? I do, and sometimes that belief comforts me and sometimes it frightens me. Do you recall Ralph Waldo Emerson's three points concerning prayer? All men pray; all prayers are answered; beware then for what you pray.

Those are broad statements but broadly true. All men pray in the sense of James Montgomery's hymn:

> Prayer is the soul's sincere desire,
> Uttered or unexpressed.

All prayers are answered, at least directionally. Tell me a man's sincere desire and I will tell you the direction his life will take, I will tell you what kind of man he will become. Beware then for what you pray—your prayer may be answered.

We pray for the brotherhood of man, not insincerely. All of us have an amiable wish that men would treat one another better. But suppose God should answer that prayer. It would mean that I should have to treat men—Jew and Gentile, black and white, people right in my neighborhood whom I find it hard to like—not with condescending politeness but as I treat my own brother; that I should not only have to act toward men as though they were my brothers but to feel toward them as though they were my brothers. Do I really want God to answer my prayer for the brotherhood of man? Am I prepared to treat men as my brothers?

We pray God to make us honest. Most of us are honest up to a point. We pay our bills. We seldom tell a lie unnecessarily. Yet all of us who try to face the truth about ourselves know how much insincerity, hypocrisy, deceit, sham, humbug there is in us.

Sometimes I wonder how, if God sees us as we are, he manages to love us. How can he help feeling contempt for us, frauds and fourflushers that we are? With some our falsity takes the form of laying claim to knowledge we do not possess, with some of paying lip service to principles (like the brotherhood of man) which in our hearts we forswear.

Society is cursed with affectation. Politics is so full of skulduggery we do not even expect a candidate to take his party platform or his campaign promises seriously. It is a penitentiary offense to obtain money under false pretenses, so from this we carefully refrain. But how many other things are obtained under false pretenses—titles, honors, offices, university degrees?

The life of many of us must appear to God as one continuous lie. We say things we do not mean, express emotions we do not feel, praise when we secretly condemn, try a hundred times a week to make people think we are other than we are.

"God, make me honest." But wait a minute. Do I really want to give up my pet pretensions? Do I really want to do what an honest man must do, be what an honest man must be?

We pray God to make us clean, to give us the inner purity Christ demands of his disciples.

"Create in me a clean heart, O God." But think what it means giving up! Do I really want to get rid of the unclean images and imaginings with which I tease myself, the secret lusts I love and hanker for even while I loathe and despise?

Or am I like St. Augustine, who tells us in his *Confessions* that he prayed, "God make me pure—but not yet"? Do I really want to do and do without what one must do and do without to be clean not only behind one's ears but between one's ears?

This is the third risk of prayer: the risk of having our prayer answered.

During the war we learned the expression "calculated

risk." Our military leaders took calculated risks because they knew that wars are not won by playing safe. The day came when they had to sail their landing craft across the Channel and storm the Normandy beaches, knowing well the risk, the fearful cost that must be paid, for only so could the foe be beaten.

Calculated risk is an element in effective living. Anyone who has ever become sufficiently dissatisfied with his moral status to want to do something about it, anyone who has seriously tried to improve his character, to change his habit pattern, knows that it is no kid-glove undertaking. We have to take hold of it with the rough hand of a man who is in earnest, who is undeterred by the prospect of blood, sweat and tears, for only so is moral victory won.

God give us grit to run the risks of prayer: the risk of seeing ourselves as we are, the risk of becoming more like Christ, the risk of having our prayer answered.

✠

Prayer

Infinite and eternal Spirit to whom our spirits are akin, we come to thee because we are unsatisfied and dissatisfied without thee. The ways of finding excitement we know well. We come here to find the path to inner peace. We have tried to find it in change of circumstance when what we should have sought was change of character. We have blamed our failure to find it on our environment when we should have blamed it on ourselves.

Save us from self-deceit as we bow before thee; from making any prayer we are not ready to have answered; from praying to be clean when we are not really trying to make a clean break with what stains and defiles our lives; from praying to be honest when we are not prepared to abandon the shams, subterfuges, insincerities which make our lives a long lie; from asking forgiveness when we are unwilling to accept the condition on which forgiveness becomes possible—a forgiving spirit toward others.

For our indolence and sloth, our selfish disregard of others' rights and needs, our turning aside from opportunities to help, for the harm we have done and the good we have failed to do, forgive us and help us to forgive ourselves.

Teach us how to make the future better than the past has been, how out of the threads of our familiar duties and common days to weave a tapestry of enduring beauty. May every experience that comes to us, whether of joy or pain, give us new insight into life's meaning and bring us closer to thee. Alike when the way is sunny and smooth and we rejoice like a strong man to run a race, and when the way is dark, rough, uphill and we are weary and faint, be thou our guide and stay.

Because of our knowledge of life's difficulty, our realization that we need a strength beyond our own, we pray for our brethren who likewise are in desperate need of thee: those whose vision has faded; those for whom life has lost its savor but who nevertheless plod doggedly along, faithfully performing life's duties; those who struggle for self-control but lose it at critical moments; those whose beloved cause them pain—all such we commit to thee. Remember those who are forgotten, neglected, unloved; and help us to remember them. To thy divine compassion we commend the sick and those in sorrow, thou skilled physician of our bodies and our souls: thou canst save and thou canst heal.

Beyond our spoken prayers we bring the thoughts that we can hardly put into words: our inarticulate longing for a closer walk with thee, our unvoiced gratitude for the goodness and mercy that have followed us all our days, our deep desire that thy will be done on earth as Jesus Christ has made it known—all these we lift to thee in his dear name. Amen.

XV

Alone, Yet Not Alone

ON THE LAST NIGHT of Jesus' life he said to his disciples, "The hour is coming, indeed has come, when you will be scattered, every man to his own, and will leave me alone." These words, recorded in John 16:32, show us how he who entered so fully into our human experience entered into this most poignant experience, the sense of life's loneliness.

"The hour has come when you will leave me alone." It was the hour when he needed them most. He never craved human sympathy and understanding as he did on this night when all else was being taken from him, when he was summoning up all his resolution, all his resources, all his reserves of power to meet the grim ordeal before him. But this companionship was not given him. The same night he spoke these words one of his little company betrayed him, another denied him, the rest forsook him and fled. He had to tread the wine press alone.

In this final, tragic solitude he entered into the common human experience. For we too go through the deep waters alone. As long as we are in the shallows we have company enough. But in the very hour when we most long for the blessed human touch on which we all so piteously depend, it fails us. We come into the world one by one. We go out of it one by one. Through all the journey from cradle to grave, the deepest, hardest experiences that come to us we have to meet and pass through alone. "Space is ample, east and west, yet two cannot walk abreast."

When Jesus went into the garden that night, the eleven accompanied him to a certain point; then eight stayed behind and the three who were closest to him went a little farther; then even they stayed behind and he went on by himself into the moonlit shadows to wrestle and to pray. So with us all when the agony of life closes in on us: beyond the kind faces of our friends, beyond the pitying glances of our neighbors, beyond the friendly jostling and camaraderie of the crowd, beyond men's praise and blame we go alone. Gregarious creatures that we are, the herd instinct deeply implanted in us, this loneliness of life is one of its bitterest experiences and one of the hardest to bear.

Think with me of three kinds of loneliness we all know. If I do not speak of the most obvious kind—the loneliness caused by parting from those we love—it is not because I am unaware how large a part in life this plays nor how many there are who know full well the heartache that kind of loneliness brings.

The first kind is caused by our inability to understand others and make ourselves understood. Only a little can we enter into one another's lives, share one another's sorrows and joys, really commune with one another. We are each shut up in his own shell; it is hard for us to get out and for others to get in. We are ships that pass in the night and try to signal each other in passing. Often the signals are misunderstood, for we signal chiefly by words and sometimes words mean one thing to one person, something else to another; opaque and ambiguous they are, bungling interpreters of the heart and mind.

Is it any exaggeration to say that this inability to understand one another is the cause of more unhappiness than almost anything else you can name? Fathers do not understand their children, children their parents, wives their husbands, husbands their wives, while all the time—here's the pathos of it—every one of us is hungry for companionship and comprehension.

We want to enter into others' lives because we do not need to think long to perceive that what we are we are because of our relationships. We are dependent on one another for self-realization, self-completion. The merchant cannot be a merchant alone. He becomes a merchant only as there are those from whom he can buy and those to whom he can sell. The teacher cannot be a teacher by himself. He becomes a teacher only as students come to him to be taught, just as a preacher becomes a preacher only when he has a congregation to preach to. We are totally dependent on others for the fulfillment of ourselves. If this is true in these casual and professional relationships, how much more in the central and mystical relationships—parent and child, husband and wife, lover and beloved.

So true is it that personality is developed, yes, determined by its relationships that we cannot conceive of personality in isolation. Is not this the real basis of one of the church's historic doctrines, the doctrine of the Trinity? The realization that God himself, if he be personal, must have society; there must be relationship in the Godhead. Therefore the great thinkers of the church have asserted that God is one substance, one being, manifesting himself in three *personae,* three relationships: God the creator and sustainer of the universe, the Father; God revealing himself in human life, the Son; God immanent in his creation, working in and through and with all cosmic forces, all natural law, but chiefly in and through the souls of men, the Spirit—and these three persons in one substance, enjoying perpetual, unbroken communion with one another.

Never think of the doctrine of the Trinity as something to be ashamed of and apologized for. Never think it does violence to the idea of monotheism when rightly understood. May I use a crude analogy? If you press it, it will be ridiculous; if you don't, it may be helpful. I am the father of my children, the son of my parents, the husband of my wife. My personality, what I am today, has been largely determined by these three central, mystical human relationships. If any of the three had been denied me, so that I had never known what it is to be a husband or a father or to have a father, I should be a different man. I am a father, a son, a husband. But I am not three men—only one. This grotesque analogy helps me in my thinking about God. I think of the Trinity not as a theological formula but as a dignified and reasonable attempt to interpret and describe God in the only way in which personality can be interpreted and described—in terms of relationships.

What we are we are because of our relationships. Only through others can we realize ourselves. The irony of it is that with this deep dependence on one another we so rarely and imperfectly understand one another, we can enter but a little way into one another's lives. This maladjustment is one major cause of life's loneliness.

Another (but one foreign to the experience of Jesus) is the

isolation caused by the sense of sin. I am aware that this expression, the sense of sin, sounds quaint and archaic. The new psychology tells us that we ought to get rid of the old, prescientific word *sin* and speak rather of the sense of imperfection, of incompleteness, or of a complex, a mental disease caused by two conflicting instincts and the resultant repression of one. I do not mean to disparage the new psychology, which is extremely interesting and not without its humorous aspects—some of its exponents take themselves more seriously than a mere preacher would dare to do. But the experience of which I'm thinking is more accurately described by that ugly little Anglo-Saxon word our fathers used in a day of blunter speech than ours.

Sin is not imperfection nor immaturity nor error nor disease—not if you're careful to use words in their proper meaning. When a man knows what is right and proceeds to do what he knows is wrong, knows what is honest and does what is dishonest, knows what is kind and does what is cruel, knows what is decent and clean and does what is filthy and degrading and vile, that's sin.

Sin brings its own punishment. One of the punishments it brings is isolation. It isolates a man from himself, his own true self, the man God meant him to be, the man he knows he ought to be, so that his personality is no longer unified and harmonious but divided, distracted, torn apart. One part of him loathes and despises what another part hankers for. And until he makes a clean break with his sin (a hard thing to do—how seldom we do it!—but it can be done) he can never live on friendly terms with himself.

Even more essential to happy and effective living than the ability to get on with other people is the ability to live on friendly terms with ourselves, because we can never get away from ourselves. If you can't get along with the people where you live, you can move elsewhere. But you'll find you've taken yourself along, and the people there will seem no more friendly unless and until you're on friendly terms with yourself. But you can never be on friendly terms with yourself as long as one part of you loves and hankers for what another part hates and abhors. Sin divides a man from himself.

Moreover, sin isolates a man from his fellows. As long as he has something he must conceal, dark corners where he dares not let in the light, he can never be a good companion; never give himself to another in that complete self-bestowal, that spontaneous, uncalculating outpouring of thought and feeling which is the summation of friendship, because he must be on his guard. How many a husband is there, do you suppose, who would like to love his wife as he knows she deserves to be loved, with that fullness of sympathy, that forgetfulness of self which transforms the marriage relation from a physical union into a spiritual bond, but can't do it because there are too many things in his past she mustn't know? How many a mother wants to love her children as she knows they ought to be loved, with an utter self-abandonment and self-impartation, but can't do it because she must be on her guard?

Do you know what it is to dream that your sin, which you thought you had hidden so carefully, had been found out and to wake up in a cold sweat with an awful sense of degradation and the feeling that you can never show your face again? That experience tends to make a man secretive, taciturn, morose, so that he isn't a good companion and people aren't keen about having him around. This is the second bad thing about sin: it separates a man from his fellows as well as from himself.

Finally, sin isolates a man from the moral order of the universe. For there is, as Matthew Arnold said, a power outside ourselves which makes for righteousness. As long as the paths of righteousness are the paths we walk, this august power is on our side and at our side. As soon as we run athwart the moral order of the universe, the stars in their courses fight against us. All the great tragedies of literature, from Aeschylus, Sophocles and Euripides to Shakespeare, Goethe, Ibsen and Eugene O'Neill, are built with unvarying monotony around this theme, that when a man defies the moral law the universe arrays itself against him.

We speak sometimes of the struggle for righteousness. A struggle it is, and the adversaries are many. But it is nothing to the struggle against righteousness, when we pit our puny strength against the moral order of God. The pleasures of sin are no doubt enticing. But the price a man pays is too high: he separates himself from his own true self, he estranges himself from his fellows, he cuts himself off from God. The sense of sin is a second major cause of life's loneliness.

One more kind of loneliness, and this the Lord Jesus shared: the loneliness which comes to sensitive, reflective, imaginative folk. Wherever I go I find sensitive, reflective, imaginative folk in every walk of life, people who want to put their lives on the highest plane they can reach and keep them there and find to their cost that they can't do it and still accept the crowd's standards and go the crowd's way.

The trouble with being popular is that popularity is sometimes due to an easy acquiescence in the crowd's practices, the crowd's point of view. The trouble with many of our companionships is that they are based on superficial, insignificant things—like a fondness for the same kind of sport or entertainment. Some are based on nothing deeper than a fondness for the same kind of drink. "Men descend that they may meet," said Emerson, "they meet on the basis of their common indulgences." A sour saying, too often true. We find it easier to come together and be congenial on a low level than on a high. If you want company more than anything else, if you want to be "hail, fellow, well met," then be commonplace, run with the crowd. But if you want to live your life on a different plane from that of the crowd, you must expect to be lonely, as sensitive, reflective, imaginative folk have always been.

Dr. Leighton Parks, who was associated with Phillips Brooks on the staff of Trinity Church, Boston, once heard a man boast that he had known Phillips Brooks intimately. Said Dr. Parks, "No one ever knew Phillips Brooks intimately." If you read Brooks's sermons, you will find in them such an understanding of human nature—the heights to which it can rise, the abysses to which it can sink, the divine depths of human love and sorrow—as you will find almost nowhere else. With unerring precision he puts his swift and sensitive finger on the human heart and says, "Thou ailest here." Phillips Brooks understood men; men never understood him. Among the crowds who thronged to his ministry he walked a lonely way.

The same was true of Lincoln. He was the pilot, the conscience, the voice of an age he understood better than it understood itself. As Emerson said, "The pulsebeats of twenty million Americans beat in him." He understood his countrymen; his countrymen did not understand him. We're just beginning to understand him now, but in his lifetime he was a lonely, solitary, infinitely pathetic figure. Why? Because in ideals, in character, in motives, he lived so far above the crowd.

The Lord Jesus knew this loneliness. There is something ironic in the story of Palm Sunday, when the people strewed branches before him and acclaimed him king, while he rode silently, steadily toward his doom. He was a king, but not the kind of king they were acclaiming. Their thoughts ran in one direction, his in another. The crowd understood Jesus and what he was trying to do that day not at all.

Nor is this surprising when we recall how little he was understood even by those who knew him best. One of the saddest incidents in the gospel story is of how, after all the pains Jesus had taken to teach his disciples the nature of the unseen, eternal kingdom for which he lived and worked and died, James and John came to him—trying to get ahead of the rest—and asked, "Lord, give us the seats at your side when you come to your kingdom." I can imagine the rueful look on his face, the little ache of disappointment in his heart as he said to Philip at their farewell meal, "Have I been with you so long, and yet you do not know me?" The Son of Man walked the lonely way.

If you want to live a life that is significant and high, there is no escape from this kind of loneliness. All you can do is accept it as part of the price you willingly pay for the privilege of living the kind of life you want to live. It's worth the price. You walk alone, but ever and again there come moments of insight, flashes of understanding to illumine and to cheer your lonely way.

A final thought and I'm done. There is One and only One

who can relieve life of its loneliness, One and only One who can abide with us always: the One who made us, whose heart beats in sympathy with ours, the infinite and eternal Spirit to whom our spirits are akin, from whom we come, to whom we return, the One to whom all hearts are open, all desires known and from whom no secrets are hid; the One who reaches down and wrestles with us in the conflict; the One who loves us through all our sins, will love us out of our sins as soon as we come to ourselves and say, "I will arise and go to my Father"; the One who is ever the comrade of the aspiring spirit, the lonely pilgrim in the upward and difficult way; the One who walks with us through all the fiery furnace of our lives; the One to whom we can flee as a bird to the mountain, who can keep us secretly in his pavilion from the strife of tongues; the Friend that sticketh closer than a brother, who "so cares for each one of us as though for him alone and so for all as though all were but one."

This was the solace, this the secret of the Lord Jesus as, despised and rejected of men, he walked serene and confident his lonely way. It was this which enabled him to say as the final darkness fell upon him, "The hour is coming, indeed has come, when you will be scattered, every man to his own, and will leave me alone; yet I am not alone, for the Father is with me."

✠

Prayer

Were we to wait till we were worthy to come to thee, we should never come. Were we to wait till we were profound enough to speak to thee with wisdom and understanding, we should be forever silent. It is often when we feel least worthy that we are most impelled to speak to thee. It is then we reach past the things we do not understand to clasp the hand of One who understands us. We come here because, like the prodigal in the familiar story, we need thee, because the world with its tinsel glitter has failed to satisfy, because having abused our liberty and squandered our time and gifts, we have manhood enough left to want to return to our Father's house, believing that not because of our worthiness but because of our need and thy pity thou wilt come to meet us, saying no word of reproof but only, "Welcome home, my son."

Over many pathways we have come, out of divers needs. Some of us need guidance, for we cannot see what lies ahead. Illumine our path and give us strength to walk in it without stumbling. Some of us need confidence, for we are timid and self-distrustful. Show us that though we can of ourselves do nothing, we can do all things in him who strengthens us. Some of us need humility, for we are prone to think too highly of ourselves, too meanly of others. Show us the good in others we often fail to see, the evil in ourselves we often overlook and which adds to the sum of the world's sordidness and confusion. Some of us need comfort, for we are lonely and forlorn. Walk with us when our path leads through the dark valley, thou Good Shepherd, thou Friend that sticketh closer than a brother. But come to us not only to guide, rebuke and encourage but to summon us to a worthier life than the life that is now ours.

We thank thee that thou dost rally us to stand up to life's difficulties; that when we have to face danger, unsuspected reserves of courage and energy come to our aid; when trial puts a long-continued strain upon us, we develop a capacity to endure we never knew we possessed; when disaster brings the blow we long have dreaded, we find underneath, supporting and upholding us, the everlasting arms. Therefore we can face whatever the morrow may bring, confiding in the promise that "as our days, so shall our strength be." We thank thee that we do not come of a race that falters when the fighting grows heavy but one that has fought and won a million battles and in the process built up a stout heart and an iron will. We thank thee above all that we are not alone in a troubled world; that we have an unseen Ally who reaches down and wrestles with us; that therefore we may look for the coming of a better world; that laying strong hold on thee, we may strive to overcome the evil in ourselves and in the world, upheld by the promise that our labor is not in vain in thee.

Sit beside us, strong Son of God, as thou didst sit at the wellside with the woman of Samaria, giving us of the living water whereof if one drinks he shall thirst no more. Sit too in the councils of those whose decisions will make or break the world's peace, giving them patience, magnanimity, sincerity, confidence in a dawn when the fear and despair which shadow men will be dispelled, the barriers which divide and estrange men be broken down; when we shall realize that we are children of God, all of us, made for fellowship with thee and one another and shall bring our social and political institutions into line with this, our true nature and destiny;

when the earth shall be full of the knowledge of the Lord as the waters cover the sea.

We ask it in his name who is our peace, who came to proclaim peace to those who are far off and those who are near, through whom we have our access to thee. Amen.

Benediction

The benediction of God rest upon his people in every land, of every tongue. The Lord meet in mercy all who call upon him by whatever name or sign. The Lord comfort all who suffer and mourn, both near and far away. The Lord bless us and keep us and grant us his peace. Amen.